CAMP OVEN COOKING

THE COMPLETE AUSSIE GUIDE

Larrikins on the Loose
PETE LORIMER • MUZ HARTIN • JACK LORIMER

WP

Published by:
Wilkinson Publishing Pty Ltd
ACN 006 042 173
PO Box 24135, Melbourne, Victoria, Australia 3001
Ph: +61 3 9654 5446
www.wilkinsonpublishing.com.au
enquiries@wilkinsonpublishing.com.au

[f] WilkinsonPublishing
[◎] wilkinsonpublishinghouse
[𝕏] WPBooks

A catalogue record for this
book is available from the
National Library of Australia

Title: Camp Oven Cooking — The Complete
        Aussie Guide
ISBN(s): 9781925927733 : Printed — Paperback

[f] The Great Coronavirus Camp Oven Cook Off
[f] larrikinsontheloose
[▶] Larrikins On The Loose, Camp Oven Cooking

Check out more of Muz's poems
www.murrayhartin.com
[▶] Murray Hartin
[f] Murray Hugh Martin

Section Photographs: Peter Lorimer
Design: Michael Bannenberg

Printed in China

CONTENTS

Introduction

G'day social-distancers, larrikins, sneeze-evaders and cough-dodgers.

When the country went into pandemic lockdown in March 2020, I was on the hunt for something to break the boredom of isolation in my Newcastle apartment. A bloke was going mad.

After yarning to my son, Jack, in Gunnedah, who was also going stir-crazy, we decided to launch a camp oven cook off via videos and texts on our phones—a little bit of friendly banter and an excuse to sample a cold beer.

For years he had been trying to out-fish, out-shoot and out-cook his old man with very little success.

On Sunday, 29 March 2020, I set up a camp kitchen on my fourth-floor apartment veranda using butane burners while Jack stoked up his backyard fire pit. The scene was set for the inaugural showdown.

Ribbing the hell out of each other all afternoon about how good our camp ovens were going, the videos, antics and language was certainly not for publication ... but we laughed that hard we had lipstick on our ears.

I brewed up a succulent red wine lamb shanks number with an assortment of seasonal vegetables and damper while the young bloke crafted what he dubbed 'A Fine Red Wine and Garlic Beef Stew'. We posted a few pics of the prep, the cook in the camp oven and plate-up to Facebook and Instagram.

That's the day we woke up a sleeping giant. A few mates contacted me during the following week asking if they could join in and the next weekend we cooked with 20 enthusiasts. It grew each week and on 14 April my wife, Tracy, and daughter, Molly, launched a Facebook

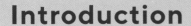

page, The Great Coronavirus Camp Oven Cook Off, so everyone could post their creations and recipes.

At the time of publication we had more than 12,000 members from all states in Australia and followers from overseas.

The rules were simple: post your prep pics (ingredients), photos of the camp oven on the cook and then a plated-up frame of your finished creation.

Each week I set a cooking theme. Some of those have been: Cook Something From The Water, Something With A Bone In It, Shank It, Chilli Ring-burners, Sweet Treats, Vegie Patch, Pies & Pastry, Pizza, Dumplings & Damper, Stuff It, One Pot Wonders and Australiana for Anzac Day, just to name a few.

During these tough times I also lost my great mate Stuart Gavin Percy. We dedicated one of the cook-offs to him called Stew For Stu. The response was nothing short of incredible.

There have been hundreds of incredible posts each week and some mind-blowing recipes which have gone viral.

Aaron Thompson's potato bake in a whole pumpkin went off the charts with more than 5,000 shares. Every week since, people have been trying to emulate his champion dish and Jason Harris posted a picture of his 109.3kg pumpkin asking members how many spuds he would need to fill it. Outstanding!

Leanne Smith's whole apples stuffed with chocolate and caramel sauce wrapped in pastry caused mayhem in the comments section of the page.

Cathy Riley and Jillian Tudgey take the prize for outstanding preparation pictures every week. They build fires in different outdoor locations and set up tables, cutlery and candles near lagoons and in paddocks.

Cathy even made a scarecrow! Unbelievable. Check it all out on the Facebook page.

We've also had our fair share of disasters posted on the page and Bert Steele takes top honours so far. After nurturing a chicken curry for five hours, slaving over the hot coals, stubby in hand, his camp oven handle snapped on his way to service and his creation ended up all over his backyard. He fixed it for the following week with zippy ties, which of course melted. Good stuff Bert.

Other highlights include Luke Berry cooking a camp oven on heat beads on the roof of a high-rise building in Sydney and iconic bush poet Murray Hartin's Great Coronavirus Camp Oven Cook Off poem which we launched live for our page around a campfire. If you want more of Muz's yarns, grab a copy of *Fair Crack of The Whip*.

A few of our overseas followers and cook-off enthusiasts are having a tough time understanding our Australian lingo. Lillian Parenteau, from Alberta in Western Canada, is constantly asking questions on Facebook trying to get a grip on what the bloody hell we are talking about.

'Can someone please explain what a larrikin is?'

'What is a cough-dodger?'

'In Canada a Jap Pumpkin is called a squash!'

Classic stuff.

You larrikins can view all of the posts, the poems and the videos on the Great Coronavirus Campoven Cook Off page on Facebook.

Stay tuned you campfire-loving larrikins and May The Camp Oven Gods Shine Down On You All.

Peter Lorimer

Australian Camp Oven History

If you research the history of the camp oven in Australia, the only thing for sure you will end up is confused.

The oldest and most sought-after ovens are Furphys and Metters, both believed to be manufactured in the late 1800s. There are plenty of arguments online about the origin of the camp oven with some saying Furphy ovens were not crafted until the 1960-70s. If you read the history on Furphy Camp Ovens, the company claims it patented cooking ovens, a firebox for ovens and cooking apparatus in 1891. To put it bluntly, who cares about dates, they are both great camp ovens and if you have one, don't sell it.

One thing's for sure, there would have been more than one starving drover in the early 1900s

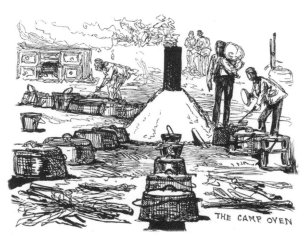

Sketches in camp from the *Illustrated Australasian Sketcher* April 11, 1883.

if not for the trusty cast iron cooking apparatus. While the drovers did the hard yards pushing the cattle, they wouldn't have got too far without the cook and the trusty packhorse loaded to the eyeballs with tucker and camp ovens.

The camp oven is a big part of Australia's history, if you haven't had a feed out of one, get busy, you won't be disappointed.

Most store-bought camp ovens are now manufactured in China and come in sizes including 2 quart, 4.5 quart, 9 quart and 12 quart (a quart is close to a litre).

Back in the day, Furphy camp ovens were made up to 20 quart but you nearly needed a small crane to lift them. The most popular Metters camp oven was a 12 inch, hence the name 'Metters 12'.

Above: Metters 12 Camp oven.

Below: 20 quart Furphy Camp Oven.

A note from Muz

G'day folks, Muz here.

I first met Pete Lorimer when I was a young, inexperienced journo back in the late '80s pumping out stories for the *Northern Daily Leader* newspaper in Tamworth.

Pete was a bit younger but a lot better and he was writing and snapping pics as well for *The Namoi Valley Independent* just up the road in Gunnedah.

A mutual love of rum, laughs and good times meant we were always destined to cross paths.

So I come to this book as a bit of a ring-in, given the whole caper was started by Loz and his son, Jack.

Loz rang, told me what was going on, explained how a two-man camp oven cooking duel between he and Jack had, at that time, exploded into 5,000 people getting on Facebook to join the fun and asked if I could knock up a poem to commemorate the occasion.

No dramas.

We organised a get together at Jack's in Gunnedah, I drove from Moree, Loz and Trace motored in from Newcastle, we had a great night around the campfire, debuted the new poem and partook of the best pork crackling I'd ever had, courtesy of Loz.

I was speaking to publisher Michael Wilkinson on the way down, he asked if I'd written anything new lately and I gave him the spiel about The Great Coronavirus Camp Oven Cook Off. He said, 'That could be a book'.

And so here we are.

I had always thought camp oven cooking was like some secret organisation where you needed a five-year apprenticeship before they even let you near a fire. But like most cooking, it's really about getting the right ingredients, doing a fair bit of chopping up, getting the right amount of heat and not adding too much of anything, particularly chilli. You can always add more but it's bloody impossible to take it out.

The hero ingredient for a good camp oven is the coals. You need good wood and hot coals—unless you're using a gas-burner of course. There are different schools of thought but generally you get a good bed of coals away from the fire, place your oven on, get it hot and then apply coals to the lid—especially if you want super-crackle crackling.

And the big thing to remember is: recipes are only a guide. If you don't like chilli or you don't like mushrooms, whack something else in. You can swap things in and out, you just have to taste as you go. Splash in a bit of Worcestershire, toss in a spoonful of minced garlic or ginger—there aren't too many rules.

But, as I said, I'm only a blow-in, a novice. Still, I did manage a couple of cracker seafood chowders straight off the bat.

The magical thing of this whole caper is, at the time of writing, 12,000-plus people have jumped on The Great Coronavirus Camp Oven Cook Off bandwagon and they're having a ball. It's brought families together and given them something fun to do during lockdown—the imagination in the recipes sent in has been nothing short of remarkable.

Loz had to school everyone in the art of photographing, filing and transferring high-resolution pics and recipes. It did test the big fella's patience for a bit but it was worth the effort.

And we also have to acknowledge the huge contribution made by Loz's better half, Tracy, and daughter Molly in establishing and managing the Facebook page.

Pete's live posts announcing the theme of each weekend's cook-off were one part instructional, three parts comedy. The whole package is gold. What started out as a simple plan to beat the pandemic boredom between a father and son has provided a ton of enjoyment for people around Australia and on foreign shores. That's got to be a good thing.

I hope you enjoy the book.

(PS If you don't like fires or have an aversion to gas burners, you can prepare just about all of these fantastic recipes in your kitchen using conventional ovens, stove-tops, slow cookers or pressure cookers—but it's not nearly as much fun.)

Murray Hartin

Restoring a rusty camp oven

G'day larrikins, burnouts, turnouts and cough dodgers. Here is a little tutorial on how to bring back the 'cast from the past'.

In my 23 years on the planet I've been fortunate enough to spend my childhood around a campfire and camp ovens on the riverbank. The old man has taught me every-thing there is to know about that life. But I can tell you, he didn't teach me anything about bringing the old rust bucket cast iron camp oven back to life. He is as handy as a small saucepan when it comes to hands-on stuff.

Righto let's get into it. The items and utensils you will need are recommended but not essential:

• A real good camp chair
• JBL flip 4 speaker for a real good track
• A generous quantity of your favourite phlegm cutters

Essential

Roll of aluminium foil
Salt
Paper towel/clean rag
Jug of water
Cooking Oil
Canola oil cooking spray
75mm Multi-Thread Stainless Steel
Crimped Wire Cup Brush (wire wheel)
on a drill for really bad rust
A positive attitude

The last oven I restored was a 70-year-old Metters 12. They're like a page 3 camp oven with a Furphy on the front cover. You start by taking all surface rust off with a wire wheel. It takes time but is essential to the rebirth of the oven. Once the bulk of the rust is off, give it a good hose out with clean water and then dry off with paper towel or a clean rag.

Take your roll of foil and tear off a generous amount and scrunch it up. Rub all of the camp oven with the foil both inside and out—the aluminium foil reacts with the cast bringing smaller surface-rust out. By this stage you should be ready to crack another cold one and continue the process.

Now it's time for a bit of heat—open flame or a gas burner, it doesn't matter. Burn the camp oven dry and get it hot then pour a cup of water in and place the lid on to steam. Boil until the water has evaporated. After it has evaporated, wipe the camp oven out with paper towel.

Next get your salt and pour in the base and wipe around the sides. Use a lot of salt, enough to cover the base. Turn the heat to low and let it burn for two hours.

After two hours, pour a jug of water in and let it boil for half an hour or so. Once it's boiled, take it off the heat and cool down. Give it a good hose and dry off.

By this stage you've had a few beers and the camp oven is looking all right. Coat the camp oven inside and out with oil and a pinch of salt and heat up for about 15–20 minutes. Let it cool down, empty and wipe dry with paper towel.

Once clean, burn hot and add one cup of water and let it boil dry. Wipe out again and this time give it a good spray with oil.

After all of that, you'll be a cracking contender for the Great Coronavirus Camp Oven Cook Off.

May the camp oven gods be with all you larrikins, burnouts, turnouts and cough-dodgers.

And like the old boy says, 'cook low and slow'.

Cheers.

Jack Lorimer

Get set to cook

You don't have to have a roaring campfire in the outback to knock up a superb camp oven. During our Great Coronavirus Camp Oven Cook Off on Facebook we have had larrikins and cough-dodgers cook up on apartment verandas, in sheds and even on the roof of high-rise buildings in the city.

Some choose to use heat beads but the quick, no fuss way is to use butane gas burners or burners attached to cylinders. Whichever way you decide to go, the secret is to cook on the lowest possible heat, the longer the better.

It's easy to get set up for under $100. The essentials include a butane burner, which can be purchased at camping stores, supermarkets etc. for around $25, while a carton of 12 butane cylinders can be bought at Big W for $16 and will last you weeks.

Camp Ovens range in size from 2 quart to 12 quart but a good all-rounder is a 9 quart ($50–$70 depending on quality). Remember you can half fill a 9 quart camp oven but you can't extend a 4.5 quart.

Other great additions to make your cook more enjoyable is a camp oven lid lifter, oven mitt, butane burner wind guard, a stainless steel trivet to lift roasts off the camp oven base and a good old fashioned can of canola spray for cooking and seasoning after use. Anyone can brew up a mouth-watering camp oven dish anywhere, anytime.

THE GREAT CORONAVIRUS CAMP OVEN COOK OFF

Murray Hartin, 9 April 2020

There's this bloke, I know him well,
A photo/journo, mad as hell
And, yeah, I've drunk a lot of Bundy with this man.
Pete Lorimer's his name,
Camp oven cooking is his game
And a few weeks back he came up with a plan.

He rang his son in Gunnedah
And said 'This might sound bizarre
'But Jack my boy I really think it's time,
'You think you're cooking's pretty cool
'So let's draw swords and have a duel,
'Take some photos and we'll post it all online.'

Well it's created quite a buzz
From the cities to the scrub,
Camp oven sales are going through the roof
As more people draw their swords,
Fan their fires, jump on board,
There's nothin' light, we're talking overproof.

It's The Great Coronavirus Cook-Off
And while it's time that virus took off
We've gotta make the best of what we've got,
So have a crack, get inspired,
Go outside and light a fire,
Grab some meat and throw it in the pot.

They've been used Australia over,
For the likes of jackaroos and drovers,
RM Williams, Jackie Howe, the deal was real.
No KFC or Maccas
For these seasoned Birdsville Trackers,
Just a humble oven made of iron or steel.

Now from Humpty Doo to Yorkey's Knob
There's crazy cookers on the job,
What they're shovin' in their ovens's outa sight,
Trout and ducks and bangers,
One truckie cooked some Vegie sangers
And by 'Vegie', well, I'm talking Vegemite!

How's that for Aussie tucker?!
And now all them other truckers
Can feel their cookin' fingers sorta itchin'.
No doubt they'll jump in too
With Magpie Pie or Rabbit Stew,
Nothing's off the menu in this kitchen.

Combine Red Chilli, Jalapenos,
Chicken stock, Tequila, vino,
Curry, spuds and just a hint of meat
But make sure you're near a dunny
Or it won't be very funny,
This Humdinger Ringer Stinger packs some heat.

So join the lawyers, teachers, brickies
And the doctors chuckin' sickies
Just so they can get in on the act.
This new Camp Oven Cordon Bleu
Makes Masterchef look amateur,
12,000-plus have joined the team and that's a fact.

It's open slather, chicks and fellas,
All you Jamies and Nigellas,
This camp-oven cooking gig is Number One,
Still, take care, don't play the fool,
Obey the social distance rules
But that don't mean you still can't have some fun.

Take your photos, crop 'em, file 'em,
Send to The Lunatic Asylum
With your recipes to tell us what it is
And if your tucker's not too crook
You could end up in the book
But geez the competition's pretty stiff.

So I bow down to my mate,
What you've done is bloody great
Lorimer you're a legend don't you know.
You've put smiles on lots of dials
That spread for bloody miles,
The Great Coronavirus Cook-Off, what a show!!

WARNING

Camp oven cooking is infectious—once you start, you'll find it incredibly difficult to stop.

Recipes in this book are a guide only, add or delete ingredients to craft your own masterpieces.

The beauty of camp oven cooking is working on instinct, throw what you want in the cast iron pot when you want. Let the oven do the hard work while you share a few tall tales around the campfire while nailing an ice-cold beer with mates.

May the Camp Oven Gods watch over you and always remember, a slow **HEAT** is the secret to brewing tender **MEAT**.

STUART GAVIN PERCY
1967–2020

In April 2020 we lost a great mate—Stuart Percy, aged 53.

It came as a shock to all who knew and loved him and as a tribute to him, we titled a theme in our Great Coronavirus Camp Oven Cook Off 'Stew For Stu'.

The response to the weekly cook-off was outstanding and the 'One Pot Wonders' came flooding on to our Facebook page with a plethora of heart-felt comments.

Stuart Gavin Percy was one of the all-time greatest larrikins I had the pleasure of being associated with for more than 40 years and there is not a day that goes by I don't reflect on the great times we had—camp oven cooking, pig chasing, fishing, laughing and going toe-to-toe with a chilled carton of VB Beer.

Great days, miss you mate.
Peter Lorimer (Loz)

Stu passed away on Monday, 6 April 2020, aged 53 years. Dearly loved partner of Sarah. Much loved father of Dan and Lachie. Adored son of Tony (dec) and Noreen. Son-in-law of Alister (dec) and Val Ingall. Likable, loving and larrikin brother to Diane and Nerieda and brother-in-law of Daniel, Angus and Kim and Hannah (dec). Best mate to Mark and cherished uncle to Kelly, Laura, Claudia, Alex, Aidan, Lauren, Kylie, Lilly and Kallan.

The Stuart Gavin Percy Memorial Plaque

Brad and Linda Gallagher are huge supporters of The Great Coronavirus Camp Oven Cook Off and, like Loz, were great mates with the late Stu Percy.

In Perc's honour, they created a magnificent Memorial Plaque awarded each month to worthy participants in the weekly cook-offs, be they camp oven chefs or avid supporters.

Crafted from a beautiful piece of polished cedar, the plaque features a mini replica camp oven above a shield displaying crossed wooden spoons.

Absolute Gold!

SPIRIT

There's a beat beneath the Olgas, out there near Uluru,
Spreading south right to the Bight and north to Kakadu.
Radiating to the shoreline there's a pulse from east to west,
That defies true definition, this strange feeling in your chest.

It's the Spirit of The Dreamtime, it's the sweat of pioneers,
It's the Rainbow Serpent's teachings of more than 40,000 years.
It's the clash of many cultures, the recipe's unique,
Reflected in our actions, what we do and how we speak.

It's the scent of eucalyptus, it's lamb chops on the barbie,
It's ANZAC Day and two-up down the pub with Uncle Harvey.
It's a nice fresh batch of lamingtons, whatever takes your fancy,
The everlasting stars that lit up the night for Clancy.

It's the right to have opinions, all open for debate,
It's the foreign-looking kid asking 'Owyagoin' Mate?'
It's the footy, it's the cricket, it's every type of sport,
On the oval, in the water or the backyard tennis court.

It's the Royal Flying Doctor, it's names like Cobb & Co,
A pie with sauce, an ice-cold beer, the farm, the surf, the snow.
It's billy tea and damper by a fire of gidgee coal,
A sunrise champagne breakfast where the colours touch your soul

Like a Namatjira painting that takes your breath away,
It's little bits of speech like 'okey dokey' and 'g'day'.
We spread the word in far-off countries but the thrill we get for free
Is when we touch down on the tarmac in our land that's girt by sea.

Sure we sing that daggy line when we stand up with the crowd
In a sea of Green and Gold 'cause we're Aussies and we're proud.
It doesn't matter what you're wearing when you're belting out that song,
Designer suits or riding boots or double-plugger thongs.

Just sing the words with passion, perhaps a little bit off key,
And you'll know The Land Down Under is the only place to be.
Beneath The Southern Cross, it's fair dinkum and True Blue,
A Golden sprig of wattle, the Boxing Kangaroo.

It's Slouch Hats and Akubras, the sweat-stained Baggy Green,
Hard Knock Schools and PhDs and all things in between.
It's a great big bunch of clichés which sometimes hide the fact
When there's hard work to be done we hook in and have a crack.

We unite in times of tragedy, fire, drought or flood,
Drop the tools and join the fight, maybe spill a bit of blood
For a neighbour, for a stranger, for a battler, for a mate,
That's the Spirit of Australia, that's what makes this country great.

So protect her and respect her in all you say and do,
Be proud you are Australian and make sure she's proud of you.

Murray Hartin

STEW FOR STU

Camp Oven Beef Bourguignon

The word bourguignon comes from a French dish that is similar to a beef stew but has a few variations and much more depth in flavour. A classic bourguignon has a strong presence of red wine which does cook out, so the kids can enjoy this great hearty winter meal.

1.5kg chuck steak, cut into cubes
3 tbsp plain flour
Salt and pepper
2 large onions, chopped
2 carrots, chopped
2 celery stalks, chopped
100g bacon, diced
300g button mushroom, diced
750ml bottle of red wine
1 beef stock cube
1 tbsp brown sugar
2 tbsp tomato paste
2 bay leaves
2 thyme sprigs
2 tbsp olive oil

Note: Best served with creamy mashed potato and crusty sourdough bread.

Dredge the beef in the flour, salt and pepper to coat. Heat olive oil in a camp oven and cook off the beef for 4–5 minutes. Transfer browned meat to a bowl to rest and lightly fry the onion, carrots, celery, bacon and mushrooms for 5 minutes until soft.

In a separate bowl pour in a splash of red wine and add the beef stock cube, sugar and tomato paste, mix to form a paste. Add this to the onion mix in the camp oven and pour in the remaining red wine. Bring to the boil then stir in the bay leaves and thyme. Turn the heat right down and simmer for 2–3 hours stirring every 10-15 minutes.

If you want a thicker stew, cook the last hour with the camp oven lid off. Serve on a bed of mashed potato and season with plenty of pepper. The longer this brew bubbles away over the coals the more flavour is produced.

Lamb Casserole

3kg lamb, cut into chunks
4 carrots, cut into chunks
4 potatoes, cut into chunks
2 punnets of vine tomatoes
Splash of red wine
About 6 mushrooms, sliced
Bacon, sliced
Bay leaves
Rosemary
Cumin
1 packet French onion soup mix
Seeded mustard
Garlic
1 lemon, zested
1 onion
About 6 cups beef stock

Have your camp oven warm. Coat the Lamb in plain flour and put it in the camp oven with everything else. Add the stock just to cover. Cook for 2–3 hours depending how hot you have it, the slower the better. Add whatever greens you want when just about ready. Serve with pasta or rice.

Cheers to Stu.

There's A Curried Roo IN My Stew

500g kangaroo, diced

2 onions, roughly chopped

2 packets of Hot Pot Curry Casserole Base

1 tbsp curry powder

4 carrots, roughly chopped

2 capsicums, diced

6 red hot chillies (to taste), roughly chopped

1 can peeled apples

1 packet of frozen corn and peas

Black pepper

There's nothing better than a good feed of Roo and this recipe is simple and requires very little preparation. The Kangaroo might be an Australian icon but there are millions of them wrecking farmers' fences, eating their crops and smashing into cars all over the country ... so what I'm trying to say is, don't worry about eating the tender little buggers.

Brown the Roo and onions in the camp oven on slow heat.

Combine the curry casserole bases and curry powder with two litres of water, mix well and pour into the camp oven.

Add the carrots, capsicum, chillies (I use six small red chillies but it's up to you), apples and frozen peas and corn. Simmer until you're hungry or the beer runs out. (Warning: Keep one beer on ice to wash down the chilli burn as this dish is best hot as hell.)

Serve on a bed of rice or mashed potato.

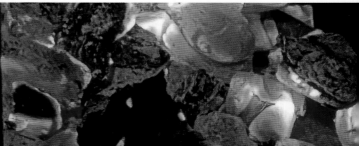

Curried Snags in a Hurry

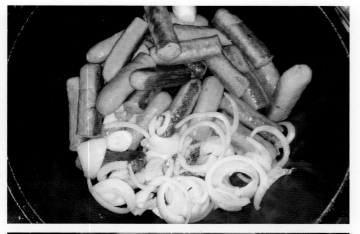

12 thin sausages

2 brown onions, halved then thinly sliced

2 Masterfood curried sausages recipe base

2 cups milk

1 tbsp curry powder

1 can sliced apples

1 small packet of frozen vegetables (your choice)

6 potatoes, peeled, boiled and mashed

Canola oil spray

Black pepper

Worcestershire sauce

Brown the sausages and onions in a camp oven (half-cook on slow heat).

In a bowl combine the curried sausage recipe bases with the milk and curry powder (or to taste). Stir well and tip the mixture into the camp oven along with the canned apple slices.

Cook slowly for one hour then add the frozen vegetables. Simmer for about the time it takes you to nail four stubbies of VB.

Serve on a bed of creamy mashed potato with a suggestion of Worcestershire sauce and black pepper. Eat until you hurt and then switch beverages to an iced-up Bundy Rum and Ginger Beer.

Warning: If you start to burp up curry, go to bed.

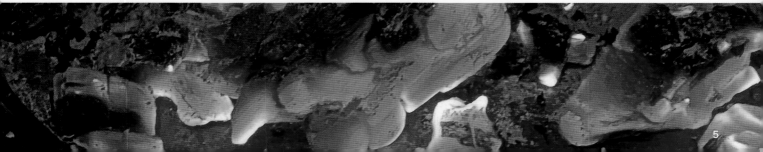

Lozza's Famous Lamb Neck Curry

This recipe is for a 9 quart camp oven, halve the recipe for a 4.5 quart or double for a 12 quart. You won't need the camp oven gods for this one ... put a horn on a jelly fish.

10 lamb neck rosettes
4 onions
6 carrots
4 packets of Hot Pot Casserole Base Curry (mild lamb curry mix from the supermarket)
1 tbsp curry powder
Fresh garlic cloves
Salt and pepper
6 washed potatoes, quartered
1 can apple slices or finely sliced fresh apple (can is better with the juices)
1 bag frozen mixed vegetables
Cornflour (optional)

Put the lamb necks in a camp oven and half fill with water.

Add onions, carrots, two packets of the curry mixes and the curry powder with finely chopped garlic cloves to taste (I put 6–7 cloves in). Add salt and pepper to taste. Bring to the boil then turn down the heat and simmer for 1½ hours.

Add the potatoes, apples and mixed vegetables and the other two curry mixes. Stir well. Simmer until the meat starts to fall off the bone, the longer the better. Keep the heat low and the lid on the oven at all times unless checking or stirring.

Thicken with a cornflour water paste if needed.

Serve with rice or creamy mashed potato, a suggestion of cracked pepper and a cold stubby of VB, or a balanced full-bodied rich red wine .... be prepared to go into a cracking food coma.

Cough-dodging braised goat

1.5kg goat leg, boned
2 tbsp ghee, butter or oil
1 large onion, diced
2 garlic cloves, finely chopped
1 cup diced tomatoes
2 tbsp tomato paste
2 bay leaves
1 tbsp thyme
1 cup red wine
2–3 chillis (if using)

Cut the meat into 3cm pieces. Heat the ghee, butter or oil in a camp oven and brown the goat. As the meat browns, remove it from the oven and transfer to a plate.

Add the onion and garlic to the camp oven and fry gently over low heat until the onion is transparent.

Add the remaining ingredients, stir well and return the meat to the oven. Cover and simmer on a very low heat for around 2 hours or until the meat is tender.

Take the lid off and let the sauce thicken for around ½ hour.

Serve with pasta, rice, salad or whatever takes your fancy and enjoy a glass of red with it.

Cheers Cough-Dodgers.

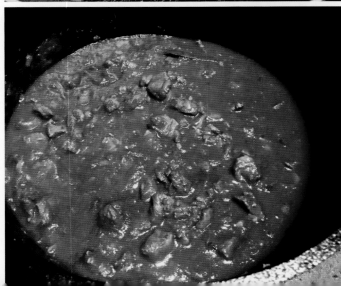

The French Man's Rabbit

2 locally sourced fresh rabbits
Olive oil
2 carrots
1 onion
1 capsicum
5 garlic cloves
3 celery sticks
¼ glass chardonnay
1 beef stock cube
1 chicken stock cube
2 bay leaves
Small bunch of spring onion

Sear the rabbit in the camp oven in a bit of oil until golden brown then remove. Caramelise the vegetables then place the rabbit on top of the vegetables. Fill with enough water to almost cover the rabbit and pour the juices from the pan into the camp oven as leftover marinade. Add the chardonnay, stock cube and bay leaves and gently boil for 3–4 hours. Garnish with finely chopped spring onions.

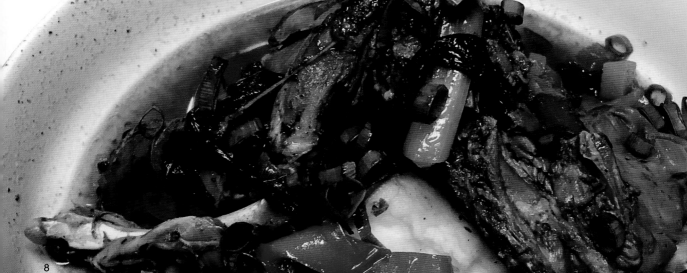

Camp Oven Massaman

Peanut oil

2kg chuck steak, diced into approx. 40cm squares

2 large onions, finely chopped

2 tbsp fresh ginger, finely grated

1 jar of massaman paste

1¼ cups of beef stock

400ml can coconut milk

2 tbsp brown sugar

2 tbsp fish sauce

6 potatoes, cut into approx. 30mm cubes

1 cinnamon stick

Roasted peanuts

White rice

Heat the camp oven and once warm add a dash of oil. Over a high-ish heat brown the meat in four batches, adding a dash of oil (about a tablespoon) each time. Transfer the browned meat to a bowl or tray and cover to keep birds and flies out.

Reduce the heat to medium and add the onions and ginger. Cook until the onions are softened then add the massaman paste and cook, stirring until you can smell it, 1–2 minutes.

Add the beef stock, coconut milk, sugar and fish sauce. Bring to the boil then add the meat and potatoes in and stir.

Add the cinnamon stick (push it under in the middle), reduce the heat to low (gentle bubble) and pop the lid on. Cook until the meat and potatoes are tender (approx. 90 minutes). Don't let the camp oven get too hot on the bottom. Sprinkle with roasted peanuts and serve with rice.

9

Beer & Beef Stew

Serves 6

750g chuck steak, cut into large chunks
Cornflour
3 small brown onions, quartered
Garlic
4 fresh tomatoes, chopped
Carrots (size of carrot will determine amount), chopped
4 potatoes, quartered
3 portobello mushrooms
1 bottle of Stout (this time it was Coopers Extra Stout)
Salt and pepper
1 tsp each of beef and vegetable stock
1 sprig fresh rosemary
Fresh parsley
Red wine to drink with meal whilst cooking

Coat the steak in cornflour and brown in olive oil in the camp oven. Remove the meat and brown the onions and garlic then add the tomatoes. Return the meat to the pot along with the carrots, potatoes and mushrooms. Mix the beef and vegetable stock into the stout then add to the oven and season with salt and pepper. Add rosemary and parsley. Slow cook for 6 hours.

Beef Chuck Stew

1kg boneless beef chuck (well-marbled), cut into 1½ inch pieces

2 tsp salt

1 tsp freshly ground black pepper

3 tbsp olive oil

2 medium yellow onions, cut into 2cm chunks

7 garlic cloves, peeled and smashed

2 tbsp balsamic vinegar

1½ tbsp tomato paste

¼ cup plain flour

2 cups dry red wine

2 cups beef broth

2 cups water

1 bay leaf

½ tsp dried thyme

1½ tsp sugar

4 large carrots, peeled and cut into one-inch chunks on a diagonal

44g small white boiling potatoes, cut in half

Fresh chopped parsley for serving (optional)

Preheat the camp oven. Pat the beef dry and season with salt and pepper.

Add a couple of tablespoons of the olive oil to the camp oven and heat on coals. Brown the meat.

Add the onions, garlic and balsamic vinegar, stir regularly to stop anything sticking to the bottom of the oven. Add the tomato paste and stir in the flour. Add the wine, beef broth, water, bay leaf, thyme and sugar. Stir and bring to the boil. Cover the oven with the lid and braise for 2 hours. Check regularly and give it a stir.

Add the carrots and potatoes. Cover and simmer for about 1 hour more, or until the vegetables are cooked, the broth is thickened and the meat is tender. Fish out the bay leaf and toss in the fresh parsley. Taste along the way and add salt/pepper etc if required.

Apricot Chicken Stew

1 onion
500g chicken breast
1 packet French onion soup
1 can apricot nectar
1L can apricots in nectar
1 capsicum
2 tsp chicken stock
Pepper

Combine all in the camp oven and
cook on a very low heat for 3–4 hours.
Serve with rice and sour cream.

Lamb chops, potatoes, carrot, sweet potato, peas, onion, herbs and spices plus slow cooking, simple but delicious. The new fire pit built for iso is the real winner!

MRS JOHNSTON'S CHOOKS

It was the harshest crime to have hit the station's books,
Some dirty low-life scum had rustled Mrs Johnston's chooks.
The robber bagged the best of them and took the rest for luck,
Forty-seven leghorns, fifteen bantams and a duck.

The pride of all the district was Mrs Johnston's flock,
From her mighty leghorn roosters to her little bantam cock.
'We'll have to put our best on this,' said Senior Sergeant Kiley,
So the call went out, loud and clear, for Stock Detective Riley.

A slow-talkin' sort of casual bloke but ruthless just the same,
He was known to all as Roundup and knew how to play the game.
He tracked a dozen Herefords from Tamworth out to Bourke
Using nothing more than instinct and a passion for his work.

And he busted up a rustling ring that spanned the eastern states,
Without the aid of partners, just a few words from his mates.
But if there ever was a case that forged his reputation,
The Homing Pigeon Hit spread his fame across the nation.

The conman Kenny Carter was the master of the scam,
For years it was his living, or in his words 'bread and jam',
By day he sold his pigeons to unsuspecting folk
And by night they'd all be home again – a money-making joke.

So, with a bank of fifty pigeons which he sold three times a week,
Ken was loving life, somewhere west of Scrubby Creek.
The hideaway was secret but with Riley on the trail
The boys back at the station knew they'd soon have Ken in jail.

With a torch taped to his saddle shining upwards from his horse
Riley rode non-stop for ninety miles to track one pigeon's course.
He dismounted at the hideaway, tied up his faithful mare,
Carter met him at the door, hands up in the air.

He stood there looking sheepish, pondering his fate,
Then Riley asked the question 'Aaaah, how ya goin' mate?'
'I thought at first,' the conman said 'that you were young and green'
'But I've gotta hand it to ya, you're the best I've ever seen.'

And now it was again that everyone conceded
To track down Mrs Johnston's chooks the Roundup man was needed.
'I aaah hear we've got a problem,' it was a voice that they all knew.
'Mrs Johnston's chooks eh, well let's see what we can do.'

Now a lesser stock detective would've headed for the scrub
But Riley's intuition took him straight down to the pub.
His *modus operandi*, at first it seemed unclear,
Then came the explanation, 'Aaah, I just wouldn't mind a beer'.

He quietly quaffed a schooner as the boys fed him the facts,
It was then that he decided on his method of attack.
He rode to Mrs Johnston's while the others drove behind
Wondering just what it was that he hoped to find.

He walked into the chookhouse, had a look around,
'Right, I'll take it all from here, thanks boys, you head back to town'.
Now they don't know what he saw, Riley wouldn't say,
He just jumped up on his horse and swiftly rode away.

Forty minutes later he was at the Kelly place
With Old Man Kelly standing there, broken teeth and crooked face,
Riley walked towards him, leaned across the gate,
Looked him up and down and said 'Aaah, how ya goin' mate?'

And as he asked the question he noticed near some trees
A single leghorn feather floating softly on the breeze.
He looked long and hard at Kelly and said 'Now you just tell me straight
'Where you may have chanced to be last night at half-past eight.'

'You see I've got the feeling you might be the type of crook
'Low enough to rustle poor Mrs Johnston's chooks.
'Now you don't have to do it but if you tell me where they are
'I just might be convinced to put away this iron bar.'

Old Kelly mumbled something, he couldn't do much more,
Then pointed out a shaky arm towards a grain-shed door.
Therein lay the missing birds which soon were taken home,
While Riley helped old Kelly pack his toothbrush and his comb.

Mrs Johnston was delighted to have back her missing flock,
All her lovely leghorns and her little bantam cock.
She said to Roundup Riley 'I truly thank the Lord
'And the only thing for me to do is offer you reward.'

Riley wasn't bashful so he thought he'd try his luck,
'I tell ya Mrs Johnston, I wouldn't mind a duck.'
Riley got his dinner and his reputation grew
But he never shared his secrets with the other boys in blue.

Just how he solved his cases was a mystery to all
But if you start out stealing stock, well, you're bound to get a call.
You'll see this bearded gentleman leaning on your gate,
He'll look you up and down and ask 'Aaah, how ya goin' mate?'

Murray Hartin

PLUCK IT

Bacon-Wrapped, Apricot Cheese-Stuffed Tur-Duc-Ken

Boned-out size 19 chook
Boned and skinned duck
Turkey breast
Block of apricot cheese
500g bacon rashers

Bone the chook and skin and bone the duck (keep the carcasses). Lay the chicken meat on the bench skin down then lay the turkey breast and duck breast on top of the chicken.

   Add the apricot cheese stuffing and roll it up as tight as possible (get an extra pair of hands to help). Make sure you pull the skin around to seal off any escape points for the stuffing. Pin together with metal skewers.

   Lay the bacon rashers in an X pattern in a greased rectangle cake tin (use long rashers and let them hang over the edge of the tin). Slap the bird roll in the tin on top of the bacon (seam side down). Wrap the bacon over the chook skin so it's covered (refer to photo).

   Place the tin on a trivet in a large pre-heated camp oven then grab another beer and cook the bugger. Cook on low heat for 3–4 hours. Enjoy!

Garlic, Lemon and Thyme Chicken Drumsticks

8 garlic cloves, peeled

Grated zest of 4 lemons

2 tsp fresh thyme leaves

1½ tsp salt

½ tsp ground black pepper

Extra virgin olive oil

12 chicken drumsticks

½ cup dry white wine

1 cup chicken broth

Put the garlic, zest, thyme, salt, pepper and ½ cup olive oil in a food processor or blender and blend to a paste.

Rub the paste on the drumsticks and place in the camp oven (pre-heated with ¼ cup olive oil) with the wine and broth. Cover and cook for 1 hour or until the drumsticks are cooked through. Serve with the juices from the camp oven poured over the drumsticks.

Stuffed Turkey

Slivered almonds

3 bacon rashers, chopped

1 brown onion, chopped

2 tbsp cranberry raisins

Olive oil

Texas Steak Rub spices

1 Quast (Tamworth) boned turkey

Broccoli

1 chicken stock cube dissolved in 1½ cups of water

1 tbsp cornflour (to thicken gravy)

Wine (red or white depending on your preference)

Roast the almond slivers either in the bottom of a hot camp oven or a pan until brown, turn frequently to prevent burning. Once the almonds are brown add the bacon, onion and cranberries with a splash of olive oil. Sprinkle in a liberal amount of Texan Steak Rub spices and cook until the bacon is slightly crispy and the onions are clear, then set aside to cool to use as stuffing in the wrap.

Lay out the wrap and spoon the stuffing onto it then wrap into a tube with both ends folded in (like a burrito).

Spread open the boned turkey and lay the stuffing wrap into the middle, fold the turkey around it and then tie the turkey up with cooking twine. To give the turkey the Coronavirus spikes, cut off some broccoli florets, slicing the stem at an angle. Then with a narrow knife stick holes into the turkey and before you pull out the knife slide the stem end of the broccoli down the knife blade into the turkey then remove the knife, leaving the broccoli sticking out of the turkey. Continue this until the turkey looks like a Coronavirus spore.

Put the camp oven on a thin layer of hot coals (good hardwood coals from Red Gum or Iron Bark will provide good heat). Place a cake rack in the camp oven to hold the turkey off the base, then put the turkey on the cake rack.

Pour the chicken stock into the camp oven and top up with some water or wine (red or white) until the liquid is just below the cake rack. Put the lid back on and shovel a small amount of coals onto the lid.

Cook for about 20 minutes then remove the lid and check on how it is cooking. Top up the liquid to just below the cake rack level, replace the lid and add coals if the cooking is too slow. Continue to cook for about one hour, lifting the lid and adding liquid to the stock as required. Don't let this simmer dry, this liquid keeps the turkey moist and makes great gravy at the end.

If you have a meat thermometer you want the temperature to get to about 68–72°C, then your bird is done. Once cooked remove the turkey and cake rack from the oven then add the cornflour as needed to thicken the gravy. Add salt and pepper to taste, carve up and enjoy!

Beer Can Chicken with
Beer-Battered Chunky Potato Scallops

Pretty easy, you just make a dry rub with 1 tbsp of brown sugar, 1 tsp each of garlic powder, dried tarragon, smoked paprika and ½ tsp each of salt and chilli powder. Bit of olive oil rubbed into the chicken and then the dry rub. Pour a quarter of one can of beer into the pot then shove the can up the chicken's bum, stand it up using the legs to stand, like a tripod. I reckon 45 minutes will do. Cheers!

Pulled Chicken Tacos

1.5kg chicken breast
1L chicken stock
1 can crushed tomatoes
3 x taco seasoning packets
1 jar of salsa
Chilli (to your liking)
Capsicum
Onion
Corn

Add the chicken, stock, tomatoes, seasoning and salsa to a camp oven and cook slowly for around one hour. Add the vegetables and pull the chicken apart using two forks. I left the lid off to thicken up the sauce at this stage. Serve with salad and sour cream on hard or soft tacos.

Pluck It, Let's Have Chicken Maryland Tonight

When time isn't on your side for a slow cook in the camp oven, this dish always does the trick and is very simple to prepare. This serves two hungry people but can be doubled to feed four (you may need a 12 quart camp oven and three jars of the creamy mushroom recipe base).

2 chicken Marylands

Olive oil

2 onions, sliced

10 button mushrooms

Finely sliced garlic cloves (to taste)

1–2 jars of Chicken Tonight Creamy Mushroom recipe base

4 potatoes

1 tub of sour cream

Baby carrots

A handful of fresh green beans

1 tbsp honey

Fry off the chicken Marylands in the camp oven with a splash of olive oil, continually turning on low heat until the chicken is three quarters cooked through (15–20 minutes).

Add the onions, mushrooms and garlic and lightly fry off for 5 minutes before pouring in the recipe base, or two if you really like it extra creamy. Simmer gently for 20 minutes or until the chicken is cooked through and tender.

Serve with boiled potatoes and sour cream, baby carrots with a suggestion of drizzled honey and green beans. Garnish with parsley sprigs and salt and pepper to taste and maybe even a splash of Worcestershire sauce.

Roast Chicken in Salt Crust

4½ cups (675g) plain flour
½ cup (160g) cooking salt
1 tbsp thyme leaves
1 cup water
2 eggs, lightly whisked.
1 (about 1.8kg) whole fresh chicken
2 fresh bay leaves
4 sprigs fresh rosemary
1 lemon, thinly sliced
6 sprigs fresh thyme
40g butter
4 garlic cloves, bruised, thinly sliced
Vegetables or salad of choice to serve

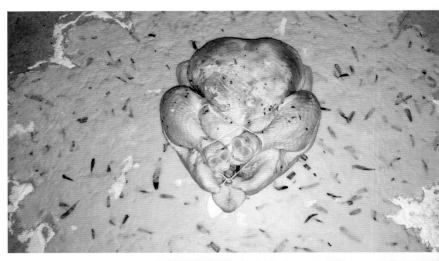

Place the flour, salt and thyme in a bowl. Add the water and egg and stir until well combined. Knead on a lightly floured surface for 2–3 minutes or until smooth. Shape into a ball and cover with plastic wrap. Place in the fridge or esky for 30 minutes to rest.

Rinse the chicken cavity under cold water. Pat dry inside and out with paper towel. Place the bay leaves, rosemary, half the lemon slices and half the thyme sprigs in the chicken cavity.

Placing the chicken breast side up, carefully lift the skin with your fingers, working it loose from the neck down to the thighs. Place the garlic, butter, remaining lemon slices and remaining thyme under the skin. Loosely tie the legs together with kitchen string. Brush with olive oil and season well with salt and pepper.

Roll the dough out on a lightly floured surface large enough to fit over the chicken. Place over the chicken and seal around the edge.

Place in a camp oven on a trivet and cook for around 2 hours on a fairly low heat so as not to burn the bottom of the crust. Remove from the camp oven and set aside for 15 minutes to rest.

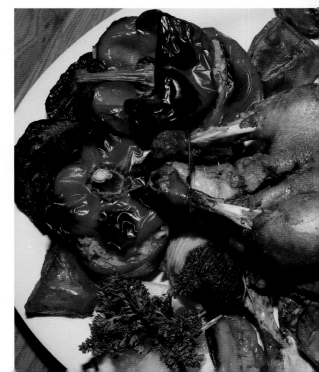

To serve, use a large sharp knife to break open the crust, discarding any crust once cracked. Serve chicken with baked vegetables, fresh greens, carrots and gravy or whatever you desire.

Duck It, Balsamic-Glazed Duck Sounds Great!

Whole fresh duck
Salt and pepper
6 garlic cloves, chopped
1 sliced lemon
Butcher's twine
Balsamic glaze
Your choice of vegetables to roast
Baby peas

Note: This is best cooked in a 12 or 16 quart camp oven depending on the size of the bird and how many vegetables you want to surround the duck with. Use two smaller camp ovens if you don't have access to a 12 or 16 quart cast iron pot.

You can also brush a little honey over the duck for a sweet touch but the balsamic glaze does the trick.

Wash the duck down with cold water inside and out. Score the duck's skin on the breast in a diamond shape, making sure you only cut the skin and not into the meat. Dry the duck with paper towel and generously rub all over with salt, which will help with crisping the skin.

Place the garlic cloves and sliced lemon pieces inside the duck and tie the legs together with butcher's twine. Pre-heat the camp oven and place the whole duck on a trivet and brush the balsamic vinegar glaze all over the bird. It is important to turn the duck every 40 minutes (generously glazing each time) to rotate the heat for three hours on a slow cook with the lid on.

With two hours to go, place the vegetables around the duck with a drizzle of olive oil over them (carrots, potatoes, sweet potato, onions and pumpkin bake well in a camp oven). A good tip to get crispy skin is to load the camp oven lid with hot coals for the final 40 minutes of the cook.

Remove the duck from the oven and discard the stuffed garlic and lemons (they are no good to eat). Serve with baked vegetables and peas.

Fried Chicken

When you're out in the bush or remote camping and crave some good old fashioned junk food, check out this simple recipe to create your own version of Kentucky Fried Chicken in the camp oven.

7–8 chicken drumsticks
2 bags of Tandaco Coating Mix
1 large zip lock bag
Salt and pepper
Olive oil
9 quart camp oven
A trivet to keep the fowl off the bottom of the cast iron pot

Place the drumsticks and seasoning mix in a zip lock bag and shake the living hell out of it until all the pieces generously coated.

Heat the camp oven over medium heat, oil the trivet and toss the chicken in. Cook for 50–60 minutes, continually rotating chicken pieces.

Serve when golden brown with salt and pepper, even a suggestion of Worcestershire sauce or sweet chilli sauce.

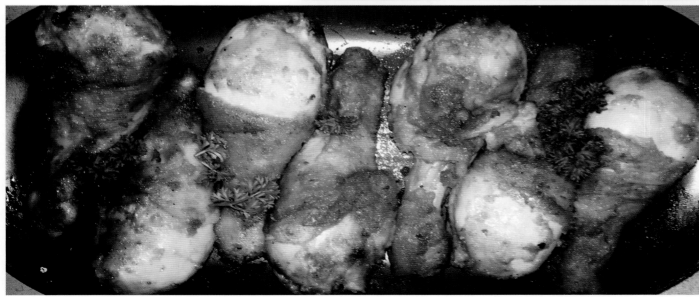

RAIN FROM NOWHERE

His cattle didn't get a bid, mind you they were fairly bloody poor,
What was he going to do? He couldn't feed them anymore,
The dams were all but dry, hay was thirteen bucks a bale
And last month's talk of rain was just a fairytale,
His credit had run out, no chance to pay what's owed,
Bad thoughts ran through his head as he drove down Gully Road.
'Geez, great-Grandad bought the place back in 1898,
'Now I'm such a useless bastard, I'll have to shut the gate.
'I can't feed my wife and kids, not like Dad and those before,
'Crikey, Grandma kept it going while Pop fought in the war.'
With depression now his master, he abandoned what was right,
There's no place in life for failure, he'd end it all tonight.
There were still some things to do, he'd have to shoot the cattle first,
Of all the jobs he'd ever done, that would be the worst.
Then he'd shower, watch the news, they'd all sit down for tea,
Read his kids a bedtime story, watch some more TV,
Kiss his wife goodnight, say he was off to shoot some roos
Then in a paddock far away he'd blow away the blues.
But he drove in the gate and stopped, as he always had,
To check the roadside mailbox and found a letter from his Dad.
Now his Dad was not a writer, Mum did all the cards and mail
But he knew the writing from the notebooks that he'd kept from cattle sales.
He sensed the nature of its contents, felt the moisture in his eyes,
Just the fact his Dad had written was enough to make him cry.
'Son, I know it's bloody tough, it's a cruel and twisted game,
'This life upon the land when you're screaming out for rain,

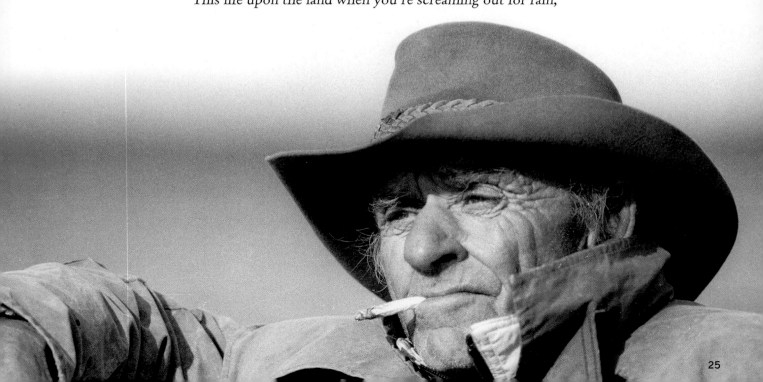

25

'There's no candle in the darkness, not a single speck of light
'But mate, don't let the demon get you, you have to do what's right,
'I don't know what's in your head but push the nasty thoughts away
'See, you'll always have your family at the back end of the day.'
'You have to talk to someone, and yeah mate, I know I rarely did
'But you have to think about Fiona and think about the kids.
'I'm worried about you son, you haven't phoned for quite a while
'And I know the road you're on 'cause I've walked every bloody mile.
'The date? December 7 back in 1983,
'Behind the shed I had the shotgun rested in the brigalow tree.'
'See, I'd borrowed way too much to buy the Johnson place
'Then it didn't rain for years and we got bombed by interest rates,
'The bank was at the door, I didn't think I had a choice,
'I began to squeeze the trigger … and that's when I heard your voice.
'You said "Where are you, Daddy? It's time to play our game
'"'I've got Squatter all set up, we might get General Rain."
'It really was that close and you're the one that stopped me, son

'And you're the one that taught me there's no answer in a gun.
'Just remember people love you, good mates won't let you down
'And look, you might have to swallow pride and take that job in town,
'Just 'til things come good, son, you've always got a choice
'And when you get this letter ring me 'cause I'd love to hear your voice.'
Well he cried and laughed and shook his head and put the truck in gear,
Shut his eyes and hugged his Dad in a vision that was clear,
Dropped the cattle at the yards, put the truck away,
Filled the troughs the best he could and fed his last ten bales of hay.
Then he strode towards the homestead, shoulders back, head held high,
He still knew the road was tough but there was purpose in his eye.
He called his wife and children, who'd lived through all his pain,
Hugs said more than words – he'd come back to them again,
Then they spoke of silver linings, how good times always follow bad,
Then he walked towards the phone, picked it up and rang his Dad.
And while the kids set up the Squatter, he hugged his wife again,
Then they heard the roll of thunder and they smelt the smell of rain.

Murray Hartin

STUFF IT

Stuffed Pumpkin Potato Bake

5 potatoes
1 sweet potato
2 onions
1 large pumpkin
400g diced bacon
2 tbsp minced garlic
300–450ml cream
500g cheese
1 tsp chilli (optional)

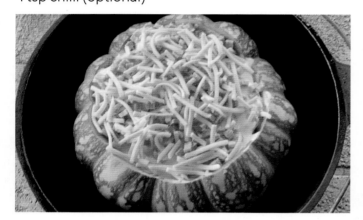

Jason Harris created a huge stir when he posted this pic on the Facebook page. He wanted to know how many spuds he'd need to replicate Aaron's recipe. At 109.3kg the answer was 'a truckload'.

Peel the potatoes, sweet potato and onions. Slice the potatoes and sweet potato about 3–4mm think and the onion a tad thicker as it doesn't take as long to cook.

Cut the top out of the pumpkin and hollow out the middle (a large metal serving spoon is ideal). Try to keep all sides and the bottom of the pumpkin even.

Place a layer of potato then sweet potato, onion, bacon and garlic in the pumpkin. Pour over some cream and repeat this process until the pumpkin is full then place half a handful of cheese over the top.

Place the pumpkin into the camp oven and sit it on a bed of hot coals. Put some coals on the lid too and keep even heat throughout cooking. Cooking time may vary due to heat and the size of the pumpkin. Use a skewer or knife to check the softness of the pumpkin and potato and when both are soft add a desired amount of cheese to the top. Replace the lid and add hot coals, cook until the cheese has browned.

Serve and enjoy.

Rolled Lamb Shoulder Stuffed with Moroccan Spiced Rice

Flatten out a boned lamb shoulder.

Finely chop some coriander, parsley and chilli. Mix in cumin and cinnamon and stir in well. Add to 2 cups of cooked medium grain rice.

Roll the rice mixture up in the lamb and tie up. Cover the lamb with olive oil and add rosemary. Cook in a camp oven on a low heat for 1½ hours.

Par boil some small whole potatoes and sweet potatoes. Get a big spoon and hit each spud until opened up. Cover with cheese and bacon bits. Cook in the camp oven then cover with sour cream and finely chopped chives.

Steam up your favourite vegies and enjoy.

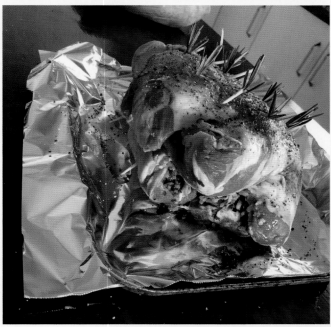

Stuffed Pumpkin

1 pumpkin
1 tbsp olive oil
1 brown onion
2 celery sticks
500g beef mince
1 green apple
2 garlic cloves
1 packet of croutons
Chopped fresh sage
Fresh thyme
¼ cup dried cranberries
1 cup chicken stock
2 eggs
Salt and pepper

Remove the flesh from the pumpkin, chop
it up and fry with onion, celery, mince,
apple and garlic. Season with salt and
pepper. Remove from the heat and add
the croutons, herbs, cranberries, chicken
stock and eggs. Spoon the mixture into
the hollowed-out pumpkin and cook for
approximately 1 hour on slow heat or until
the pumpkin is cooked through. The secret
is to keep checking it.

Baked Lemon Pork Chops
Stuffed Pumpkin

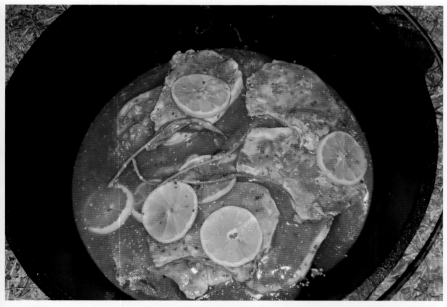

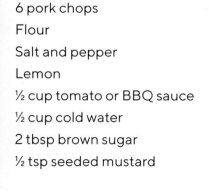

6 pork chops
Flour
Salt and pepper
Lemon
½ cup tomato or BBQ sauce
½ cup cold water
2 tbsp brown sugar
½ tsp seeded mustard

Coat the pork chops in flour, salt and pepper. Place half a slice of lemon on top of each chop. Mix the sauce, water, brown sugar and seeded mustard then pour over the chops. Bake in an uncovered dish in a moderate oven until cooked (1–1½ hours). You may need to add more water if the sauce dries out.

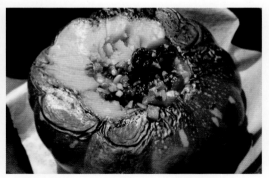

1 pumpkin
1 packet of dried apricots
Handful of prunes
5 bacon rashers
2 tbsp brown sugar
1 green apple, peeled and cut

Remove the flesh from the pumpkin, cut it up and mix it with all the remaining ingredients. Fill the pumpkin with the stuffing and cook in the camp oven until tender.

Anzac Weekend Lest We Forget Roast Chicken

I cooked two chickens for about 1½ hours with lemon, thyme and a bunch of tomatoes. I then added the vegies to bake and the greens.

For dessert I cooked a cake in the camp oven on baking paper. It was just a packet cake with canned fruit that was strained and then placed on top of the cake and baked till cooked through. It turned out perfect.

Spinach and Feta Stuffed Chicken
Creamy garlic sauce

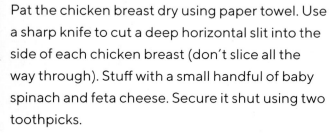

Large chicken breasts
Baby spinach
Feta cheese
Olive oil
Minced garlic
Salt and pepper

Pat the chicken breast dry using paper towel. Use a sharp knife to cut a deep horizontal slit into the side of each chicken breast (don't slice all the way through). Stuff with a small handful of baby spinach and feta cheese. Secure it shut using two toothpicks.

Combine the olive oil and garlic in a small bowl and rub all over the chicken breasts. Season with salt and pepper and set aside.

Heat up a camp oven with olive oil.

Add the chicken to a frying pan and cook for 2 minutes on each side or until lightly browned. You may need to do this in two batches if you have a small pan. Transfer the chicken to the oven and cook for a further 10–15 minutes or until cooked through. Remove from the oven and cover with foil to keep warm. Set aside for 5 minutes.

Remove the toothpicks from the chicken. Serve alongside roast vegies.

Tip: If you don't have an oven-proof frying pan then place the chicken on a paper lined oven tray and cook as per the above instructions.

Cooking cream
Minced garlic
Shallots

Measure with your heart (and tastebuds of course) Cook in pan over the fire and drizzle over the chicken.

Carpet Bag Steak

Serves 4

1 doz Fresh oysters (preferably still in the shell)
½ cup freshly chopped parsley
50g butter
4 x any thick cut of steak (preferably eye fillet)
Salt and pepper

Remove the oysters from the shell. Gently fold the oysters, parsley and soft butter together.

Turn steaks on their side and make a big enough incision for three large oysters to fit in. Fill the pocket of the steak with the oyster and butter mixture. Secure each opening of the steak with toothpicks. Cut the toothpicks so that they are the same size as the steak. Season the steaks both sides with salt and pepper. Lightly brown both sides of the steak and wrap in foil, be careful not to puncture the foil as juices will release. Gently place the steaks on a raised rack in the warmed-up camp oven and cook for approximately 10–15 minutes.

Serve with any gravy and a bed of mashed potato. Enjoy.

Beef and Mushroom Hot Pot Cooked Inside a Jap Pumpkin

1 generous sized Jap pumpkin

1kg diced rump steak

3 cloves garlic, minced

1 onion, sliced

200g mushrooms

100ml red wine

1 tbsp chicken stock

1 carrot, finely diced

1 zucchini, finely diced

Salt and pepper

1 packet French onion soup mix

Cooked bacon pieces to garnish

Cheese to garnish

Cut out the top off the pumpkin and keep as a lid. With a Texta or Sharpie, mark a dot on the pumpkin and a matching dot side by side on the lid, so that when you match the dots the lid of the pumpkin is exactly matched and secure.

Carefully hollow out the pumpkin with a spoon leaving a 10cm diameter inside the pumpkin (reserve the pumpkin for soup).

Brown the onions and garlic in a pan with a little olive oil. Add the meat until brown. Remove from the heat.

Add the vegetables and red wine to the pan with the packet of French onion soup mix, chicken stock and salt and pepper. Return to the heat and reduce the liquid to half.

Add all the mixture into the hollowed-out pumpkin. Sprinkle cheese and bacon on the top. Place the pumpkin lid back on top, place on a rack in the camp oven and slowly cook for 90 minutes. Enjoy with mashed potato.

'Stuff It' Roast Pork

200g frozen chopped spinach
1 medium boneless roast pork leg
Butter
100g button mushrooms, sliced
15g pine nuts
100g feta cheese, roughly sliced
(All stuffing ingredients are approximates
depending on size the of pork)
Oil
Cooking twine

Take the frozen spinach out of the packet
and spread out on paper towels to thaw
then squeeze the excess water out and
set the spinach aside.

   Score the pork skin and pour
boiling water over it. Dry the skin then
rub a generous amount of salt over it and
set aside.

   In a pre-heated camp oven, melt
a little butter in the bottom and cook
the mushrooms and pine nuts for a few
minutes while stirring, just until the pine
nuts are slightly brown. Remove and let
cool in a bowl.

   Place the oven back on the coals
to heat.

   Slice the pork in half (parallel
to skin) being careful to leave a few
centimetres uncut. Layer the spinach,
feta, mushrooms and pine nuts in the cut
centre of the pork. Close over and tie well
with cooking twine.

   Cook in a camp oven over slow
heat for two hours then put hot coals
on the lid to bring crackle to the crunch.
Times may vary, just keep an eye on it,
you'll know when you have good crackle
but don't overcook the pork.

Rice-stuffed capsicums

2 tbsp olive oil
2 small onions, finely chopped
3 garlic cloves, crushed
1 cup long-grain rice
1½ cups water
2 vegetable stock cubes, crumbled
2 zucchinis, coarsely grated
2 tomatoes, cut into 1 cm pieces
½ cup chopped fresh dill
Salt and pepper to taste
4 large red capsicums
Extra olive oil to serve

Heat oil in a camp oven over a medium heat. Add onions and garlic. Cook while stirring until soft. Stir in the rice. Add water and stock cubes. Bring to the boil. Simmer, covered, for 10 minutes. Remove from the heat. Stir in the zucchinis, tomatoes and dill. Season with salt and pepper to taste.

Cut the tops off the capsicums and reserve for lids. Scoop out and discard the seeds and membrane. Spoon the rice mixture into the capsicums. Place in another camp oven or clean out the one used to prepare the rice. Replace the capsicum tops.

Cook in a medium heated camp oven for about 45 minutes or until tender. Rest for 10 minutes before serving.

THE HOG WHISPERER

His name is Scotty Parker, from Meandarra way,
A rural jack-of-all-trades, never has too much to say,
Now he's pretty good with cattle, got some fairly handy dogs
But he's known as The Whisperer, the man who talks to hogs.
He's got a PhD in pork, speaks fluently in grunt,
He knows everything about 'em, inside out and back to front.
We're not talking your domestic breeds, give the man a break,
Berkshires, Large Whites, Tamworth Reds? A piece of bloody cake.
Nahh, the Whisperer likes a challenge so you know that he'll be found
Chasing filthy, feral, fetid hogs that reek and root around.
Yeah, a squealing, squawking porker that's been trapped and acting tough
Will be as timid as a lamb once The Whisperer does his stuff.
But it isn't only swine, other creatures love him too,
They're still talking 'bout the carnage that he caused at Dubbo Zoo.
See they had this female hippo that had lost her 'loving' form,
They got The Whisperer on the phone and he was talking up a storm.
They had to call him back an hour later … to get the antidote,
She'd fixed up three bull elephants, two tourists and a goat!
But it's a pig he can't forget, the biggest one he'd whispered down,
A humungous red-necked Razorback who'd terrorised a town.

Everyone was packin' death but Scotty walked straight in
To the biggest hog he'd ever seen but he just winked and gave a grin,
Then a snort and grunt and squeal, it was bloody weird to see,
He said *'Put away your shotguns, boys, he's comin' home with me'*.
It jumped up on his four-wheel-drive, completely filled the tray,
Scotty gave his snout a scratch, hopped in and drove away.
Now Scotty's dogs were kept on chains 'cause they'd rip your legs to pieces
But he said *'Nothin' holds old Razor, mate, he just does as he pleases'*.
'He's a mongrel in the garden but there is a major plus,
'There's been some thieving in the district - no one ever bothers us.
'See, he can smell annoying bastards three mile down the track,
'He'll toss his head, charge their car, not too often they come back.'
Things can happen for a reason, coincidence or fate,
Whatever it was, Scotty now had strangers at his gate.
And he'd lent his dogs to Koonta, Razor too was missin'
But The Whisperer wasn't worried, it was Razor's ruttin' season.
Now, some people look for trouble and deserve all that they get,
Enter three young mixed-up punks who didn't know it yet.
They were on the run and headed east, they'd nicked a car in Gundy
And fired up with false bravado and fuelled by beer and Bundy

They thought they'd stage a home invasion and as they passed the boundary well
They turned right at Scotty's signpost for a journey into Hell.
Scotty thought that it was Koonta bringing back the hounds
But they marched up with 22s and said 'Hit the bloody ground!'
'Just give us all your money or we'll shoot you here and now.'
Scotty said *'You dickheads, I'm a farmer, the best you'll get's a cow'.*
They decked him with a rifle butt but he struggled to his feet,
Mustered all his strength and let out a loud *'Soooooooo-eeee!!'*
Through many years of whispering hogs Scotty knew it all
And the long 'soo-ee' to Razor was a *'DANGER! DANGER!'* call.
They heard a rumble in the distance, the sound of falling logs,
'What's that?' one punk asked Scotty, he replied *'It's just my hog'.*
Well, the ground began to tremble, the head punk got the shakes,
The Whisperer warned *'Look out boys, I think he's brought his mates'.*
They rushed to the verandah, the air was full of grunt
From a mob of 57 hogs with Razor at the front!
The moon lit up the monster's tusks, his eyes were filled with hate,
Two-fifty kegs of angry bacon who'd come to save his mate!
The punks fired their 22s, they had Razor in their sights
But 22s to Razor? They were just like mozzie bites.
All it did was make him cranky, the punks were losing heart,
Scotty shook his head, said *'Fellas – that wasn't very smart'.*

The invaders now were shi-ing bricks, one began to cry,
The Whisperer said *'Hand me the guns, you might get out alive.*
'Take off your shoes, lose your clothes, when I give the word get running,
'I'll give you fifteen minutes' start – then you'll hear the grunters coming.'
Well the cops were on the spot when out the Gates of Hell they flew,
They were yelling *'Bloody pigs!'* – so they copped a flogging too.
The pig now lives a life of luxury, which upsets Scotty's bride,
I mean he's got a Five-Star sty, but the bastard sleeps inside!
And he loves his trips to town where he guards The Whisperer's truck,
If anyone tries to nick it … well, let's just say they're out of luck.
And the Razor breeding program, it's dead-set going great,
Scotty makes a bloody fortune selling guard pigs interstate!
But he hasn't lost the magic, he's still the Swinging King of Swine,
If you've got problems with a hog he can help you every time,
Don't try to tackle it yourself, you'll be headed for a fall,
Let your fingers do the walking, give The Whisperer a call.

Murray Hartin

ROASTED

Mustard and Maple Syrup Pork Belly

1kg pork belly
2 tbsp maple syrup
2 tsp whole grain mustard
2 tsp apple cider vinegar
2 tsp chopped rosemary

Pat the pork dry and score the skin then season well with salt and place on a rack with water underneath. Cook on high heat until the rind is starting to crackle.

Reduce the heat and cook slowly for an hour or so. Keep topping up the water as needed.

Combine the maple syrup, mustard, vinegar and rosemary. Drizzle over the pork, cook for another 5 minutes until the rind is dark and golden.

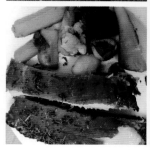

Roast Beef and Chook on a Spit

Whole chicken
Olive oil
Salt and pepper
Portuguese seasoning (optional)
Green apple
Celery
Breadcrumbs
Rind and juice of 3 oranges

Rub the chicken with a bit of oil, salt and pepper and Portuguese seasoning. Core the apple, dice the celery and stuff inside the chicken with the breadcrumbs, orange rind and juice, and salt and pepper. Tie the legs together with cooking twine to hold the stuffing in and thread the chicken onto the spit. Cook on the spit around 15cm above the coals for 1½–3 hours, depending on the size of the chicken. The chicken can dry out while cooking so baste every 20 minutes with a mixture of olive oil and lemon juice. The chicken is ready when the internal temperature is 75°C.

Roast Beef from our local, Mornington Butchery, cooked in the camp oven with potatoes, carrots, pumpkin and onions for approximately 1½ hours or until the meat is tender. Season with salt and pepper and serve with steamed Brussels sprouts, broccolini and pak choy or vegies of your choice.

Enjoyed with a few beers with the family around our homemade fire pit.

We are all loving the Facebook page you have put together.

Asado Beef Ribs

String the ribs out flat on a steel crucifix. Stand it upright and build a fire in front of it, not letting the flames touch it. Cook it on the front for 2½ hours then turn it around and cook the back for 3 hours.

Rack of Lamb and Maple Pumpkin

4 rosemary sprigs

2 mint sprigs

1 tbsp red peppercorns

2 garlic cloves, chopped or minced

3 tbsp olive oil

2 racks of 'Frenched' lamb ribs

4 pumpkin wedges

½ cup maple syrup

8 potatoes wrapped in foil

1 lemon

3 anchovy fillets

3 tbsp butter

Finely chop the rosemary and mint and mix with the peppercorns and garlic, blend together and set aside one third to put on the pumpkin later.

Rub olive oil over the lamb racks and then rub the rosemary herb blend over the lamb.

Pour the maple syrup into a bowl and add the third of the rosemary herb blend. Put the pumpkin into the bowl and mix the maple and herb blend to coat the pumpkin thoroughly.

Get the camp oven nice and hot and add some olive oil to the base. When nearly smoking add the lamb, meat side down, and sear the outside until a nice brown colour. Remove the lamb and place a trivet (cake rack) in the bottom of the camp oven, then place the lamb racks back into the oven on top of the trivet. Have the lamb racks back-to-back and interlock the ribs, this will make it easier to fit the two racks in the oven. Place the pumpkin pieces around the lamb, you can fit a couple of pieces in between the lamb racks as well.

Put the camp oven back on a bed of coals and place a shovel full of coals onto the camp oven lid. Cook for approx. 40–50 minutes depending on the heat quality of the coals.

Put the foil wrapped potatoes into some coals on the fire, turn them after 15 minutes and move to the outer edge of the coals to keep warm after another 15 minutes (push a knife or skewer into them to see if they're cooked or if they need to cook a bit longer). While the lamb is cooking, zest the lemon, finely chop up the anchovy fillets and mix together with the butter (add salt to taste) to use on the potatoes when served. Enjoy!

Leg of Lamb with Dessert

Leg of Lamb for tea which I marinated in red wine and oil then topped with garlic, rosemary and chilli and cooked for at least 3 hours. I put the carrots, potatoes, onions and tomatoes in about halfway through. I made my gravy with a bit of flour and everything that was on the bottom of the oven. The greens I just boil in some water.

Waffle Cones Stuffed with Marshmallows. Use chocolate, strawberries and whatever you want really. Wrap in foil and put in the camp oven or just on a flat surface over hot coals. You have to watch them or else they will burn fast. **Stuffed Apples.** Apples rolled in sugar then wrapped in pastry and stuffed with chocolate, caramel sauce and walnuts. Don't look too flash but they were yummy. Not so many coals on the bottom but more on top of the oven. All trial and error really.

Rib Eye Roast with Creamy Horseradish Sauce & Vegetables

Beef Rib Eye
Sweet potato
Potato
Pumpkin
Corn
Broccoli
Cauliflower

Place the Rib Eye in the camp oven with the sweet potato and pumpkin. Coat with olive oil and season with salt, pepper and rosemary. Cook on low heat for 1½ hours or until the meat is to your liking. Wrap the corn in foil and cook on the campfire. Steam the broccoli and cauliflower.

Creamy Horseradish Sauce
3 tbsp horseradish cream
½ cup sour cream
1 tsp Dijon mustard

Mix all together and serve on the side. Enjoy!

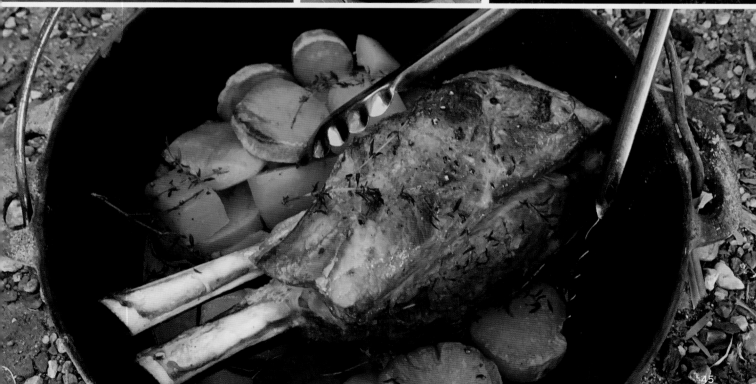

Bacon-Wrapped Venison Maple-Glazed Pumpkin

600g venison loin, fat and sinew removed
(Liverpool Ranges Feral Fallow Deer used in this
cook off)
1 cup red wine
1/3 cup raspberry vinegar (can use apple cider
vinegar instead)
2 rosemary sprigs, strip leaves and dice ½ of them
4–6 large pumpkin wedges
4 shallots, sliced into quarters lengthways
¼ cup cranberry raisins
½ cup maple syrup
40g butter
1 tbsp olive oil
6 bacon rashers (optional)
1 tbsp red peppercorns
1 tbsp sea salt flakes

The day before cooking, remove any fat or sinew
from the venison loin and soak (marinate) the
venison in the red wine, raspberry (or apple cider)
vinegar and rosemary leaves. Put it in the fridge and
turn it over after 12 hours.

Get a good fire going with hard wood that
makes good hot coals.

Put the pumpkin, shallots, 1 tsp of the diced
rosemary, cranberry raisins and maple syrup into
a bowl and mix until the pumpkin is thoroughly
coated.

Lay a shovel full of coals out beside the fire
and place the camp oven on them, then pour the
bowl with pumpkin and liquid into the camp oven
add half the butter. Replace the lid and cook for 30
minutes (or until the pumpkin is tender).

While the pumpkin is cooking, lay another
shovel full of coals out beside the fire and place a
second camp oven on them. Once it is hot, add the
other half of the butter, a splash of olive oil and when
it is foaming add the venison and bacon rashers.

Sear the venison quickly on all sides. Once seared
remove the venison and bacon from the camp
oven and set aside until the pumpkin is cooked in
the other camp oven.

When pumpkin is tender, place the
venison on top of the pumpkin and then cover
the venison with the bacon. Pour in a small
amount of the marinade juice into the bottom of
the camp oven to keep the liquid from reducing
to nothing. Put the lid back on the camp oven
and put a small shovel full of hot coals on top of
the lid. Cook for 15–20 minutes maximum.

While that's cooking, smash the
peppercorns and remaining rosemary up (with a
mortar and pestle or a hammer) and mix with the
salt to use as seasoning.

When the venison is cooked, remove the
camp oven from the coals, take out the venison
and put it on a plate to rest (10 minutes), laying
the bacon on top to help keep it warm. Get a few
spoonfuls of the glaze from the bottom of the
camp oven and drizzle it over the venison and
bacon. Carve up the venison and serve it on top
of the pumpkin and shallots. Pour the remaining
pan juices over the meat and pumpkin and
sprinkle a generous amount of the peppercorn
and rosemary salt blend over the dish and enjoy!

Pork spare ribs boiled in apple juice and brown sugar then basted with a paste of tomato sauce, chilli, brown sugar and apple cider vinegar. Loaded potatoes and garlic bread. Delicious and finger-licking good!

Cashew-Crusted Rack of Lamb

Frenched eight-bone rack of lamb

Salt and black cracked pepper

2 tbsp olive oil

2 cups cashews (whole or pieces)

2 tsp dried rosemary

2 cups breadcrumbs (panko or homemade)

¼ cup Dijon mustard

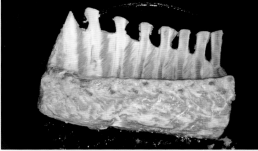

Season the lamb with salt and pepper. Heat the camp oven on a medium heat until hot. Add olive oil. Sear the lamb on all sides until golden brown. Remove from the heat and let the rack sit for 5 minutes.

While the lamb rests, place the cashews, rosemary and breadcrumbs in a food processor and pulse until coarsely chopped and well mixed. Be careful not to over-pulse or the cashews will turn into butter (or just roughly crush cashews into small bits in a mortar and pestle and stir through rosemary and breadcrumbs).

Smear the rack with the Dijon mustard and lightly press the cashew mixture on the lamb, being sure to evenly coat the entire lamb except the bones.

Place the lamb on some baking paper and lightly cover the cashew coating with foil so it doesn't burn. Return the lamb on the baking paper to a medium-hot camp oven with a trivet for 12 minutes. Remove the lid and foil then replace the lid and cook for a further 12 minutes. Serve with whole baby honey carrots, beans, camp oven roasted vegetables and gravy if desired.

Honey carrots

1 bunch whole baby carrots

2–3 tbsp Australian honey

Cut the carrot tops leaving one inch of green for presentation. Peel the carrots and par cook for 5–6 minutes in boiling water. Drain the water and remove carrots.

Melt the honey in a pan over medium heat and return the carrots to the pan. Cook, turning a few times, until caramelised to a nice dark brown.

Note: This can all be done in a camp oven or a saucepan.

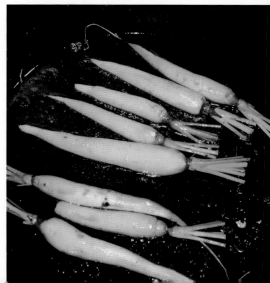

4 beef femur bones cut down the centre and knuckle ends cut off

1.5kg strip loin

1 tbsp olive oil

1 tbsp Pit Happens Texas Steak Rub spices (or spices of your choice)

1 tbsp sea salt flakes

Gravy Sauce (optional)

1 cup beef stock

½ cup chicken stock

1 cup red wine

1 punnet shitake mushrooms, sliced in half

1 leek, chopped

4 shallots, cut in quarters lengthways

3 garlic cloves, whole

2 tbsp cornflour (to thicken if required)

Have your butcher cut the femur bones in half lengthways, then cut the knuckle ends off leaving approximately a 4-inch barrel of bone and marrow.

With the strip loin warmed to room temperature, coat in olive oil then roll the meat in the spices, cover it thoroughly. Adding salt to the beef will draw out the flavours (optional).

Sit the striploin on its end then split the bones and stack them up vertically, side by side, all around the striploin with the bone marrow facing in against the meat.

With cooking twine, tie around the outside of the bones to tie them up hard against the meat, go around the meat 3–4 more times to ensure the bones are firmly in place.

If you want to have a gravy sauce, put the stock into the bottom of the camp oven. Place a round baking rack in the camp oven (if you have put in the gravy mix the rack should sit just above the liquid) and place the strip loin on top.

Place the camp oven on a layer of hot coals (preferably coals from a good hardwood such as Red Gum, Iron Bark, Mallee, Mulga or Snappy gum) and then put a layer of hot coals on top of the camp oven lid.

Cook for between 1–2 hours (depending on the heat of the coals), check the meat after 30 minutes to see how it is cooking and top up the gravy liquid if it has reduced too much. If you have a meat thermometer cook to 53°C for medium rare. This strip loin seems to cook a bit quicker than normal, the bones radiate the heat into the meat quicker than would be expected.

Once the meat is cooked, remove it and let it rest for 10 minutes.

While the meat is resting finish cooking the gravy and thicken with cornflour if required.

When ready to serve, cut off the twine and the bones will fall away. You will notice most of the marrow has disappeared as it has infused into the meat. Mmmm delicious, enjoy.

No-Fuss Ginger Beer Silverside

If you are looking to experiment with different techniques and tastes, this one is a beauty and very simple to nail. A 9 quart camp oven will handle a nice slab of corned silverside. You can nail this meal for under $25 and can serve 6–8 people.

Corned silverside
2 large bottles of ginger beer
½ cup vinegar
2 tbsp brown sugar
2 bay leaves
2 large carrots
1 onion, peeled whole
Salt and pepper

Place the meat in a camp oven, cover with ginger beer and then throw in the vinegar, brown sugar, bay leaves, carrots and onion. Bring to the boil then simmer with the lid on for 40 minutes per each half kilogram of meat.

   Drain the ginger beer from the pot, carve generous slices of tender pink meat and serve with any vegetables you fancy.

   White sauce and hot English mustard are sensational with a mountain of creamy mashed potato if you are looking for a few ideas to enhance the feed.

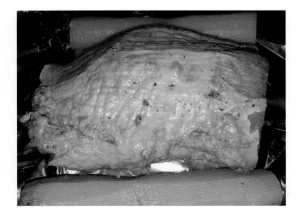

FISHIN' FOR COD

Killer, Quenten and Bloody Mick went fishin' out west for cod,
They took Reschy along as their spiritual guide, he was known as the Jamtin God.
The trek had been planned for six long months and all was now in order,
They were ready to go to The Great Beyond, just north of the Queensland border.

With a thousand yabbies, six hundred carp and a mile or more of worms
They had the bait to lure the fish and meet 'em on equal terms.
For the cod that come from The Great Beyond, near the Never Go Dry Lagoon,
Are the hardest cod in the world to catch, they don't waltz to the fishermen's tune.

Well, the four-wheel-drive was sardine-packed, the trailer stacked ten foot high
With boats and tackle and food … and grog … the boys weren't gonna go dry.
They got to the river at the crack of dawn, an eerie mist on the water,
The Jamtin God stood up and proclaimed *'Bringeth the lambs to the slaughter'*.

They set their lines, they made their camp then Killer opened a beer,
He drank a toast to a healthy catch and said *'Tell the cod we're here'*.
A tinkering bell was the first alert that the fish were on the bite
But the line hit the water, springer and all, and vanished out of sight.

Ten more went as a frenzy began, there was little the boys could do,
There was just no chance of grabbin' the lines or their hands'd be cut in two.
The rot went on for three long days, the party was spent to a man
Except, of course, for The Jamtin God, who had one final plan.

So they hooked the carcass of a flyblown ewe to the anchor from one of the boats,
The sheep had been dead for a good two weeks and stank like a thousand goats.
They secured the lot with a length of chain to an old rusty plough by a tree,
Said The Jamtin God *'If the cod breaks that he's far too good for me!'*

Well, they whistled their way to their sleeping bags, 'twas a jovial fishermen's choir
Then Quenten sang some Al Jolson songs by the flickering light of the fire.
They drifted off to the Land of Nod … but soon awoke in fright
As the murderous sound of a fish-drawn plough came thundering through the night!

The plough was headed straight for the camp, the chain was glowing red,
Gum trees snapped like matchsticks and the boys thought they were dead
But Bloody Mick, he cracked the whip and said *'Quick, get in the truck!*
'We can catch this sucker with half a chance … and given an ounce of luck.'

So they followed the plough for an hour or so 'til the fish had finished its run
Then they tied the chain to the four-wheel drive and the battle had begun.
Killer jumped in the driver's seat and with a look of satisfaction
Said *'The bloody cod's as good as caught, get ready for some action!'*

The engine roared, the tyres spun, the boys were pushing hard,
The sun came up … and the sun went down and they'd gone forward just a yard.
But they inched ahead, the cod was beat, the boys let out a cheer
As this Moby Dick of the Inland Sea he started to appear.

With a mouth as big as a block of flats, there was nothin' he couldn't swolla,
He was forty foot from lip to gill … with plenty more to folla!
Now, Killer was clockin' up overtime, the tyres were all but bald
While the others watched as the fish came out … and the river began to fall!

And all across the countryside the rivers were running dry,
From Mungindi to Shepparton the folk were asking *'Why?'*
The Darling was barely a trickle, the Murray ran hardly a drop
'Til the PM flew in from Canberra and he begged the boys to stop.

See drought had hit the country bad and they'd finally found the cause
So the boys cut loose that Super Cod to national applause!
The river levels rose again, the tragedy averted,
The fishing party headed home a trifle disconcerted.

Now, they'll tell you they've captured some big cod since
But the biggest without a doubt
Was the monster they caught but had to release
To save the land from drought!

Murray Hartin

OUT OF
THE WATER

Camp Oven Baked Trout

½ cup butter, melted
2–3 lemons, sliced
Trout (cleaned and gutted)
Seasoning (salt and lemon pepper or your favourite blend)
Olive oil
1–2 rosemary sprigs

Pour the melted butter into the camp oven and make a bed of sliced lemon for the trout on top of this.

Generously season the fish inside and outside and insert 2–3 slices of lemon. Add the trout to the camp oven and drizzle with olive oil. Chop about 2 tsp of rosemary and sprinkle on top. Cook with the lid on, on low heat for 10–15 minutes or until a fork falls through the fish with no effort. Keep an eye on it as will quickly dry out if left steaming for too long.

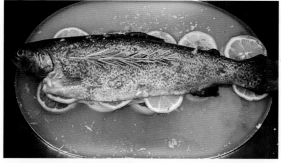

Seafood Chowder

Oil

100g smoked ham, diced

2 leeks, bottom half of stem thinly sliced

3kg potatoes, peeled and cut into small chunks

1–2 sticks celery, chopped into 1cm slices

1–2 brown onions, sliced

3 garlic cloves, crushed

1L chicken stock

Kernels from 2 cobs of corn

1 bay leaf

A few shakes of thyme

500g skinless white fish fillets (e.g. cod, snapper)

15–20 scallops (no roe)

15–20 green prawns (peeled, tails on)

12–15 mussels

500ml thickened cream

Salt and ground black pepper

2–3 tbsp chopped parsley

Sourdough/crusty bread to serve

Heat the oil in a camp oven and add the ham, leek, potato, celery, onion, garlic, stock, corn, bay leaf and thyme. Put the lid on the camp oven and cook until the potato is cooked through (2–3 hours). Give it a rough mash or hit it with a whizz stick.

Dice the fish into 2cm cubes, toss in the oven with the scallops and prawns. Add cream, replace the lid and cook for 30 minutes or until the seafood is cooked.

Add salt, pepper and parsley to taste and serve with bread.

Stuffed Rainbow Trout for Two

2 cloves freshly minced garlic

1 tbsp butter

2 whole rainbow trout

1 lemon, cut into 5mm slices and
then cut into half moons

Diced tomato and onion

1 large sprig of rosemary and parsley

Salt and pepper

Aluminium foil

Mix the garlic and butter together in a small bowl.
Divide and spread generously inside the cavities of
each trout then add the lemon, tomato and onion,
salt and pepper, rosemary and parsley.

Place 3–4 slices of the lemon inside each
fish then tightly wrap each fish in buttered up foil.

Place the parcels on a trivet (on baking
paper sprayed with canola oil) in a pre-heated
camp oven on a very low heat for approximately
10 minutes each side (depending on the size of
the fish).

Serve with homemade chunky hot chips.
(Cut potatoes into chips, par-boil for 5–10 mins
depending on thickness, dry and let cool down.
Cook in oil, deep or shallow fry, in the camp oven
until crunchy and brown on the outside.)

Mixed Seafood with Ginger and Saffron

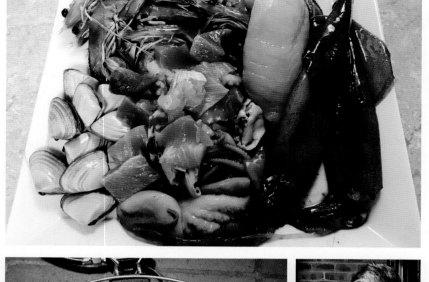

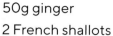

Serves 4

50g ginger

2 French shallots

250ml white wine

1 pinch of saffron

80g butter

2 squid (calamari), cut into rings

300g white fish fillet

500g mussels

300g seafood marinara

12 pippies

1 bunch of coriander, chopped

Peel and thinly slice the ginger and shallots and add to the camp oven along with the wine and saffron. Cook until the liquid is reduced by half.

Add the butter to the camp oven then the seafood. Cover with the lid and cook over low heat for 5–6 minutes. Done!

Scatter with coriander over the top and it's eating time. Serve with crusty bread warmed up and it's heaven to mop up the sauce.

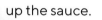

Coral Trout
Creamy Garlic Prawns

The fish

½ onion

1 chilli or chilli powder (to your liking)

1 handful of parsley

Coral Trout/ any good eating fish

Salt and pepper

1 lemon

Dice the onion, chilli and parsley, set aside. Slice cuts down the sides of the fish and rub the skin with chilli, salt and pepper. Stuff the fish with the onion, chilli and parsley mix, put it into the camp oven and cook over low heat. Cook until the slices in the side of the fish open up nice and wide. Enjoy!

The prawns

115g butter

1 garlic clove

1 tbsp plain flour

1 cup chicken stock

½ cup cream

2 tbsp white wine

½ tsp mustard powder

Salt and pepper

750g raw prawns

½ cup peas

1 tbsp parsley, chopped

Melt the butter and stir in the garlic and flour. Gradually add the chicken stock, cream and wine. Add the mustard powder, salt and pepper. Bring the sauce to the boil then add the prawns and peas and cook for 5 minutes. Stir through parsley and serve.

Curried BBQ Prawns
with Brussels Sprouts and Rice Noodles

Fresh green prawns

Garlic, minced

Ginger, minced

Oil

½ tsp curry powder

Brussels sprouts, chopped in half

Rice noodles

1 red onion

Chilli

1 tbsp sesame oil (optional but worth it)

2 tbsp soy sauce

Toasted peanuts

Lime

Shell the prawns, leaving on the head and tail.

Mix the garlic, ginger, 1/3 cup oil and curry powder in a bowl, add the prawns and Brussels sprouts to marinate and let sit for 10 minutes.

Boil a camp oven full of water and cook the rice noodles for 3–5 minutes. Drain quickly.

Finely dice up the red onion and chilli, throw in a bowl with 1 tsp each of oil and sesame oil and 2 tsp of soy sauce (add some honey if you have any). Stir the sauce through the hot noodles.

Throw the Brussels sprouts on a heated and oiled grill over your fire just above the flame and cook for 1–2 minutes each side. Throw on the prawns and cook for 40 seconds each side.

Serve topped with peanuts, chilli and fresh lime.

Seafood Paella

4 tbsp olive oil

4 garlic cloves, minced

1 large red onion, finely diced

2¼ cups risotto rice

1 heaped tsp smoked sweet paprika

¾ cup canned chopped tomatoes

6 cups chicken stock

Large pinch of saffron

10 mussels

20 shelled tiger prawns, tails
left on

500g calamari

Salt and pepper

Chilli flakes

½ cup fresh parsley,
chopped

Lemon wedges to serve

Have a fire going strong with plenty of coals. In a large paella pan add 2 tbsp of oil, the onion and garlic.

Add the rice and paprika and cook the rice for about a minute, stirring the whole time so it can soak up the flavour from the onion mixture.

Add the canned tomatoes, stock and saffron. Bring the mixture to the boil then reduce the fire and cover the pan with the lid and cook for about 15 minutes or until the rice is almost cooked.

Remove the lid from the pan and arrange your seafood on top of the rice, making sure to tuck the mussels into the mixture. Cover the pan once again and cook for about 10 minutes or until all the seafood is cooked.

Season with salt and pepper, increase the fire and let the mixture cook for about a minute or until the rice starts to brown on the bottom and gets crispy.

Top with chilli flakes (optional) and parsley and serve with lemon wedges.

Prawns, Cod and Poached Pears

Serves 4-6

Entrée: Gambas Al Pil Pil (Prawns)

1kg raw prawns
½ tsp salt
50g butter
1/3 cup olive oil
3 garlic cloves
¼ tsp chilli flakes
½ tsp paprika

Peel and devein the prawns, keeping the tails intact. Mix the prawns with the salt in a large bowl, cover and refrigerate for about 30 minutes.

Heat the butter and oil together in a flameproof dish over medium heat. Roughly chop the garlic and when the butter and oil are foaming add the garlic and chilli and cook, stirring, for 1 minute or until golden. Add the prawns and cook for 3–6 minutes or until they curl up and change colour. Sprinkle with the paprika and serve sizzling hot with plenty of bread for dipping.

Main Course: Murray Cod (a la Grand Hotel)

4 x 150g cod fillets
Plain (all purpose) flour
    for dusting
Salt and pepper
Olive oil
Butter
A pinch of finely chopped garlic
½ cup peeled and diced tomato

Pre-heat the oven to 180°C. Lightly flour the fish slices (it is always a good idea to put a little salt and pepper in the flour and have it well mixed). Add the oil and butter to the pan and when the butter is melted add the fish. Cook it lightly on one side then turn over.

Add the garlic and tomatoes. Keep cooking for 1 minute and place the pan in the oven. If the heat is gentle and the pan hot, the fish will cook and the butter will not separate. If the butter splits it looks oily, take the fish out and tip out some of the oily butter out then add in a few small butter cubes and stir them in. Cook for a few minutes or until ready. Serve at once with side dishes of boiled potatoes and fresh salad.

Dessert: Poached Pears in Red Wine

1 orange
1½ cups (375ml) red wine
3 tbsp sugar
2 cloves
1 cinnamon stick
1 lemon
4 pears, brown or Corella

Slice the (unpeeled) orange into at least 6 pieces and put in a stainless steel sauce-pan (or small camp oven) with the wine, sugar, cloves and cinnamon stick. Bring this to the boil then gently simmer and stir for 3 minutes or until the sugar has dissolved. Turn off the heat and cover the pan.

Now to the pears. Chop the lemon in half. Peel the pears and rub each with lemon to stop them from discolouring. (Leave the stalks on the pears because these look pretty when the dish is finished.) Slice a sliver off the bottom of each pear, thus enabling them to stand on their own during cooking and service.

Put the pears upright into the wine mixture, return the heat to low and cook for up to 20 minutes or until the pears are tender. Take them out of the saucepan and let them cool a little while you reduce the mulled wine/poached liquid to a saucy consistency. Strain the sauce into a jug (or leave the oranges in the sauce if you prefer). Plate the pears and pour over the sauce.

Crispy Skin Snapper with Chilli Sweet and Sour Sauce on Rice plus Calamari

Snapper, not too large that it won't fit in your camp oven

Cornflour

Squid tubes

Breadcrumbs

Onion

Carrot

Capsicum (red and green)

Broccoli

½ cup vegetable stock

¼ cup rice wine vinegar

1 tsp soy sauce

2 tbsp tomato sauce

2 tbsp caster sugar

Tin of pineapple in natural juice

Tin of baby corn

Two small chillies

Rice bran oil

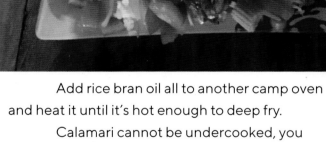

Score the snapper into 2cm cubes on both sides then roll in the in cornflour and put in the fridge. Slice the squid tubes into calamari and crumb. Use cornflower, egg and breadcrumbs (fresh or bought).

Cut the onion into chunks and dice all the vegetables into small bite-sized portions.

Mix the vegetable stock and rice wine vinegar with the soy sauce, tomato sauce and caster sugar and set aside.

Separate the juice from the pineapple and add 1 tbsp of cornflower to the juice and mix.

In a pot bring 1 tbsp of oil to heat and add the onion and carrot, sauté for about 1 minute. Add the sauce and bring to the boil. Once boiling add the rest of the vegetables and cook for 2–3 minutes then add the pineapple and the pineapple juice mixture and reduce to a simmer. Cook for 45 minutes.

Add rice bran oil all to another camp oven and heat it until it's hot enough to deep fry.

Calamari cannot be undercooked, you basically put it in for 30 seconds so it's easy to do 2–3 at a time.

Serve with lemon and tartare sauce or whatever your choice as entree.

When you are ready cook the snapper, it takes longer than you think, until it is very crispy, 4–5 minutes per fish.

Serve on a bed of rice, pour the sauce over the fish and put the vegetables around the edge and enjoy.

Liz's Salmon Smash

Mash

700g sweet potatoes
2 limes
Bunch of coriander
Jar of mango chutney
Soy sauce

Salmon

8 slices pancetta or prosciutto
4 fillets salmon (skin on)
1 tsp fennel seeds
1 lemon

Peel and slice the sweet potato and add to a camp oven on a trivet. Add a bit of water and one lime (halved and squeezed a bit). Cook until the sweet potato is tender.

Remove from the pan then cook prosciutto/pancetta until crispy. Remove that then cook the salmon on a relatively hot heat for 3–4 minutes each side or to your liking. Sprinkle with bruised/slightly ground fennel seeds during cooking. (You can also use other fish if you're like my son and don't eat salmon.)

When all cooked, put the mango chutney on the base of a serving platter, top with sweet potato (with a squeeze from the remaining lime and chopped coriander), then chopped pancetta and salmon fillets. Give it all a rough chop to combine slightly and serve with lemon wedges.

The best way to eat this (if you're not needing to social-distance or cough-dodge) is sitting around the platter and digging in with your forks.

Creamy Seafood Chowder
(The Chowder That Gets Louder)

1 medium carrot, finely chopped

5 (approx. 750g) peeled potatoes, roughly chopped

4 cups (1L) fish or chicken stock (I used 2

cups of each)

2 corn cobs

500g marinara mix

200ml thickened cream

Salt and pepper

2 tbsp chopped fresh chives

2 tbsp chopped fresh parsley

Crusty bread to serve

Place the carrot, potatoes and stock in the camp oven. Cover and bring to the boil. Reduce the heat and simmer for around 10 minutes until the vegetables are tender.

Process the mixture with a hand blender until smooth (use a potato masher, fork or handheld eggbeater if out bush). Return to the pan.

Cut the kernels from the corn cobs and add to the pot. Simmer for 10 minutes or until the corn is tender.

Reduce the heat by taking the camp oven off the hot coals for a few minutes then add the marinara mix and cream.

Stir, slowly increasing the heat without boiling, for about 3 minutes or until the seafood is cooked and the chowder is hot. Season to taste with salt and pepper.

Stir through the chives and parsley. Serve immediately with bread or damper.

Barramundi Curry with Broccoli, Bok Choy and Cauliflower Rice

A hearty and healthy winter warmer!

Garlic
Ginger
Turmeric
Fennel seeds
Coriander
Cumin
Curry powder
Red chilli
Fish sauce
Sea salt
Water
Onion
Coconut milk
Chicken stock
Broccoli
Bok choy
Barramundi fillets

Blend together the garlic, ginger, turmeric, fennel seeds, coriander, cumin, curry powder, chilli, fish sauce, sea salt and enough water to make a paste.

Sauté the onion in the camp oven and add the paste. Cook for 5 minutes then pour in the coconut milk and stock. Cover and bring to the boil.

Reduce the heat, add the fish pieces and broccoli and simmer for 7–10 minutes before adding the bok choy.

Serve with cauliflower rice.

Seafood Paella

Olive Oil

1 chorizo (Spanish sausage), cut into coins

1 brown onion, finely chopped

3 garlic cloves, chopped

1 capsicum, finely chopped

1 large carrot, finely chopped

1 tomato, finely chopped

500g chicken wings or drumsticks

1 tbsp paprika

500g diced pork

250g squid rings

500g rice (bomba or arborio)

500ml fish stock

250ml white wine

Fish fillet diced (white fish)

1 bay leaf

1g saffron thread (crush threads with salt in mortar and pestle)

1 tbsp salt

500g raw prawns (shelled)

250g mussels

½ cup frozen peas

Nutmeg (optional)

500ml warm water

Heat the olive oil in the camp oven and fry off the chorizo. Remove it from the oven and set aside for later but keep the oil and sauté the onions and garlic for 2 minutes. Add the capsicum and carrots and when softened add the tomato and stir.

Once softened add the chicken and sprinkle with half of the paprika. Add the diced pork 3 minutes later and the rest of the paprika. Cook the meat until browned and keep stirring to stop it from sticking to the pot.

Add the squid rings and cook for 3 minutes.

Add the rice and stir through quickly with the meat. Add the cooked chorizo back in and the stock and white wine, let simmer.

Add the diced fish pieces, bay leaf, saffron and salt to taste, stir through. Cook with the lid off for 10–15 minutes.

Add the prawns and as the liquid evaporates add warm water a bit at a time until the rice is 90% cooked (about 30 minutes).

Add the mussels and peas and cook for 5 minutes.

Remove from the heat, add sliced roasted capsicum pieces for colour, cover and let stand for 10 minutes before serving. 'Buen provecho!'

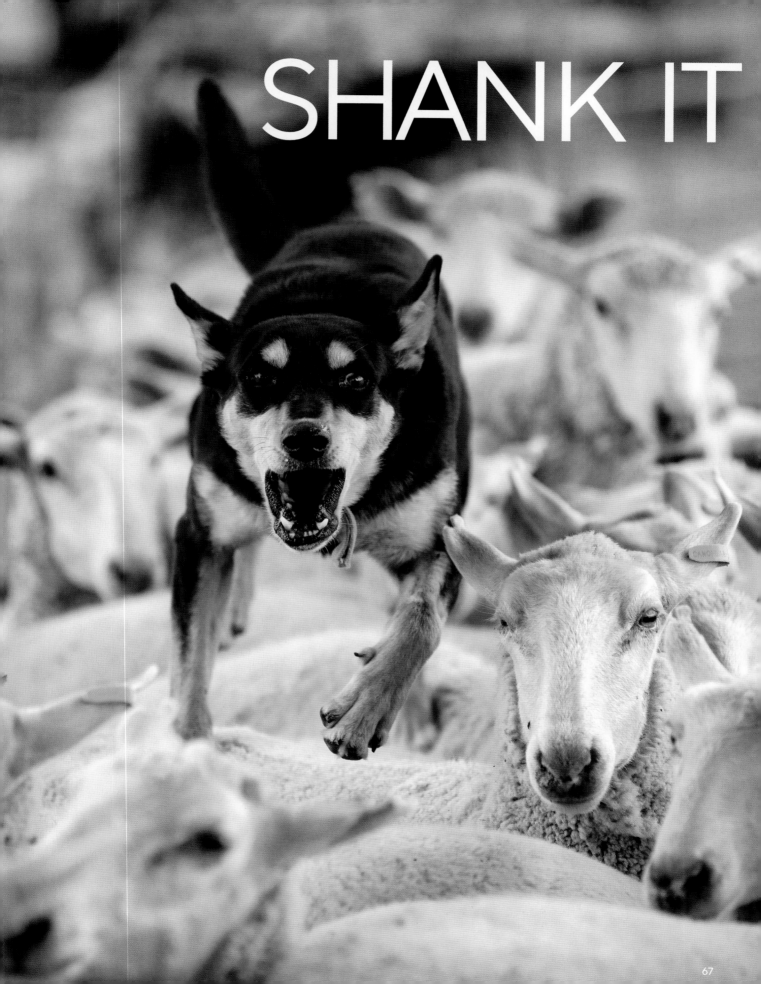

SHANK IT

FAIR CRACK OF THE WHIP

Mick, he was a bushman, he was up there with the best,
He'd been in the saddle nearly all his life
But lately things had changed, his thoughts had rearranged,
Yes, it was time that Michael found himself a wife.

So he was giving up the one-night stands and giving up the booze,
He would settle down and get himself employed
And with a sad state of remorse he sold his faithful horse,
No more the saddle life would he enjoy.

And the object of his fancy was the local schoolgirl miss,
She was pretty, she was delicate and frail,
Mick fell in head-first, the kind of love it was the worst
That womenfolk can foster in a male.

He wasn't taking any chances, he was playing all his cards
And Elizabeth McGee she was the stake,
He did all he could to win her, he'd take her out to dinner
And on Sundays they'd go walking by the lake!

Then finally the night arrived that Mick had waited for
When Elizabeth invited him for tea.
He showered, combed his hair and he had this speech prepared
'Ahh, Elizabeth, will you marry me?'

You see he knew he had to marry this young girl from the south,
She was cute and kind and every mother's dream,
Her hands were soft and gentle, she was sweet and sentimental
And her eyes they sparkled with a magic gleam.

So they shared a lovely dinner and Mick was most polite
'Though thoughts of marriage occupied his head,
So he was very much inspired when she casually enquired
'Would you like to see the etchings by my bed?'

'I'll slip into something comfortable, you go into the room,
'Take your drink and lie down for a while.'
And while she didn't look satanic, young Mick began to panic
When he saw the wicked nature of her smile.

Then she burst back through the door wearing leather head to toe!
She had stilettos on and pistols at her hip!
Towards Michael she was prowling, she was grunting, she was growling!
And in her hand she held a nine-foot whip!

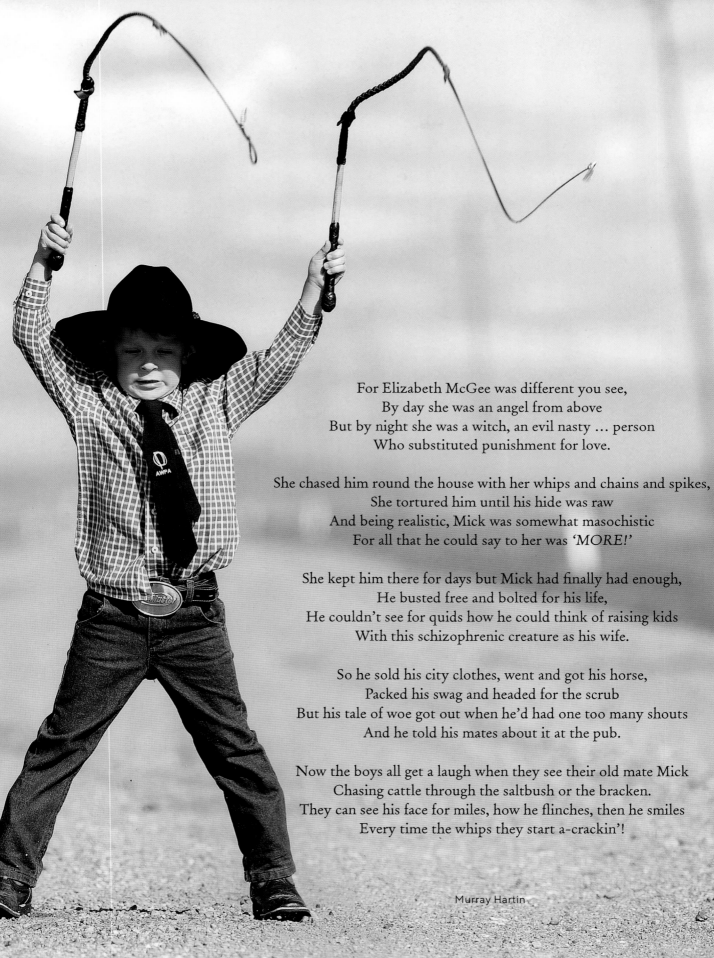

For Elizabeth McGee was different you see,
By day she was an angel from above
But by night she was a witch, an evil nasty ... person
Who substituted punishment for love.

She chased him round the house with her whips and chains and spikes,
She tortured him until his hide was raw
And being realistic, Mick was somewhat masochistic
For all that he could say to her was *'MORE!'*

She kept him there for days but Mick had finally had enough,
He busted free and bolted for his life,
He couldn't see for quids how he could think of raising kids
With this schizophrenic creature as his wife.

So he sold his city clothes, went and got his horse,
Packed his swag and headed for the scrub
But his tale of woe got out when he'd had one too many shouts
And he told his mates about it at the pub.

Now the boys all get a laugh when they see their old mate Mick
Chasing cattle through the saltbush or the bracken.
They can see his face for miles, how he flinches, then he smiles
Every time the whips they start a-crackin'!

Murray Hartin

Lamb Shank and Bacon Bone Stew

2 large carrots
2 celery sticks
2 large potatoes
1 large brown onion
2 tbsp minced garlic
2 tbsp mixed herbs
70g tomato paste
2 cups chicken stock
1 cup water
1 large lamb shank
1 large bacon bone
½ cup soup mix

Chop up all the vegetables and place in the camp oven. Add the garlic, mixed herbs and tomato paste on top. Pour over the chicken stock and water and give it a good mix through. Add the lamb shank and bacon bone and cook on high heat for two hours then cook on medium heat for 4–6 hours. For the last two hours of cooking, add the soup mix in.

Shanks and Vegies

Serves 4

Plain flour
Salt and black pepper
4 lamb shanks
Big splash of cooking oil
3 carrots, roughly chopped
3–4 large potatoes, roughly chopped
1 brown onion, chopped
6–8 garlic cloves (chopped or minced)
Leaves from 2 sprigs of rosemary, chopped
1–2 cups red wine
4 tbsp tomato paste (or 1 small tub)
4 cups (1L) beef or vegetable stock

Preheat the oven over coals. Mix the flour, salt and pepper in a bowl. Coat the lamb shanks in flour. Heat the oil in the camp oven and add the shanks. Once the shanks are browned add in the vegetables, garlic, rosemary, red wine, tomato paste and stock. Simmer for a couple of hours (stir regularly) until the meat starts to fall off the bone.

No-Fuss Garlic and Herb Lamb Shanks

Serves 4

If you don't have time to spend on preparation try this no-fuss way to brew up perfect lamb shanks in the camp oven.

Canola oil spray
Salt and pepper
4 lamb shanks
2 Masterfoods Garlic and Herb Lamb Shank Recipe bases
1–2 cups water
1 packet button mushrooms
2 tbsp garlic paste
2 sprigs of rosemary
1 can diced tomatoes
4 carrots, diced
2 tbsp tomato paste
5 potatoes, peeled and mashed

Season the shanks with salt and pepper. Spray the inside of the camp oven with canola oil and brown the lamb shanks for 10–15 minutes.

Over a low heat, add the two recipe bases and 1–2 cups of water, stir well.

Add the mushrooms, garlic, rosemary, tomatoes, carrots and tomato paste, mix and simmer on the lowest possible heat for 2–3 hours, stirring regularly.

Serve on a creamy bed of mashed potato with crusty sourdough bread. Garnish with a rosemary sprig and ground black pepper.

Baked Lamb Shanks

Two lamb shanks marinated in a mixture of red wine, oil, garlic, chilli, rosemary, thyme and lemon.

Cook the shanks for about 2 hours. Halfway through throw some vegies and tomatoes in. The tomatoes give a lovely taste to the gravy. When nearly ready cook some greens.

The meal was delish and so was the red wine, yummo!

John's Lamb Shanks

2 tbsp olive oil

4 large lamb shanks

1 cup good red wine (enjoy the rest whilst cooking dinner)

1 cup Tawny Port (save the rest for after dinner by the fire)

1 sachet 'Slow Cooker Beef and Red Wine' (McCormick's or Masterfood)

500g mushrooms, chopped

4 large carrots, chopped

3 bacon rashers, chopped

2 garlic cloves (whole)

1 brown onion, chopped into wedges

1 (400g) can diced tomatoes

6 potatoes, diced

1 tbsp chopped rosemary

Build your fire up with good hard wood such as Red Gum, Box or Iron Bark to get a good pile of hot coals. Shovel a layer of coals to set your camp oven on and heat the oven up.

Spread the olive oil on the camp oven base then add the lamb shanks to sear/brown the outside. Turn them regularly to get good even browning. Once the shanks have browned, add the red wine, port, slow cooker sachet, mushrooms, carrots, bacon, garlic, onion, tomatoes, potatoes and rosemary. (Note, you can remove the shanks first then add these to warm up before putting the shanks back in the camp oven if you wish.)

Stir and allow to slow cook for 2–3 hours, don't make the layer of coals too thick as this is a slow cook and you don't want to burn the liquid to the base, you want it to slowly simmer and cook slowly until the meat is falling off the bone and the flavours have infused. Lift the lid every 20 minutes or so to check how it's cooking and if you need to add more water as the liquid reduces.

Enjoy!

Tim's Lamb Shanks

4 lamb shanks

3–4 carrots

2 celery sticks

4 tbsp tomato paste

Splash of red wine

4 tsp crushed garlic

Paprika

Italian or mixed herbs

Worcestershire sauce

Salt and pepper

Sprig of rosemary

1kg potatoes

250g green beans

Add the lamb shanks and all ingredients except the potatoes and beans to the camp oven. Depending on the heat (160–200°C) cook for 2–3 hours. Peel the potatoes, cut and boil in salted water until soft. Steam or boil the beans until tender. Mash the potatoes and place on plates, top with the shanks and serve the beans on the side.

THE SLOUCH HAT

There's a Slouch Hat in my lounge-room,
Pristine and never worn,
Standing watch atop a globe
Dawn til dusk and dusk til dawn.
It will never go to battle,
Never ask the question *'Why?'*
But it sings to me A Sappers Lullaby.

It won't play footy by The Pyramids,
Won't taste Kokoda's mud,
Won't feel the heat of Vietnam
Nor be stained by good men's blood,
It won't trade shrapnel in the chaos
On a beach at ANZAC Cove
But it tells me quietly why the rough men go.

Men like my mate Coops,
Who gave the hat to me,
Who back the Engineers
As they clear the IEDs,
Thirty feet apart,
Treading softly, staggered file,
Under the Afghan sun they walk the danger miles.

And I've shared beers and laughs with Timmy
And I've looked him in the eye,
Heard him talk about lost mates
And I've seen a tough man cry,
Just like those who've gone before him,
And they may go on forever,
The slouch hat, well, it binds them all together.

With just a sideways glance
It can set my brain to work,
Recall the deeds of Albert Jacka,
Hear the pledge of Ataturk.
Eric Bogle sings Waltzing Matilda
And the lyrics haunt my mind
As I think of all the heroes left behind.

But the Rising Sun will not forget them
As it shines on new recruits,
Brave young men and women,
Bold as brass in shiny boots.
Duntroon and Kapooka,
Passing every test
And beneath the Slouch Hat's brim they'll do their best.

So the Slouch Hat in my lounge room,
It won't travel overseas
But it takes me on great journeys
And reminds me why I'm free.
A symbol of Australia,
No surrender, few regrets
And a shrine to those now gone,
Lest We Forget.

Murray Hartin

SMOKING, SPITTING & JAFFLES

Billy and Linc Are Smoking

They reckon they are two of Gunnedah's biggest larrikins, and they're not too far off the mark.

Billy McCann, 26, and Lincoln Smith, 21, love a good cook-off and when the Great Coronavirus Camp Oven Facebook page launched, they were grinning like fox cubs eating roo guts in long grass.

Lincoln, a boiler maker by trade, and Billy, a coal miner, both knew their way around a campfire but they thought they'd take it to the next level.

'Surprisingly, we've got heaps of hungry and thirsty mates so we needed to cater for the champions in a big way,' said Billy McCann. 'Linc and myself designed and purchased the materials to craft an Off-Set Smoker made from an old hot water system and thought we'd have a crack and manufacturing a spit at the same time,' he said.

The Smoker cost them around $1000 to build while the spit was just over a grand after they purchased the motor and spit rods from online company Flaming Coals. It took the lads just over a month to get both cookers up and burning and they lost count of the cartons of beer that shifted through the esky, not to mention the Ned Kelly Captain Morgan, while toiling away on the job.

'We had a few disasters in the initial stages but we're starting to nail the cooks now Billy is paying more attention to me,' said Linc. 'We cooked a lamb on the spit first up and while it looked tremendous on the outside, it was bloody raw when we carved into it,' he said.

The boys use hickory wood to start the smoker process and then switch to ironbark once the flavour kicks in.

'I'm blaming the Captain Morgan rum on our first few stuff ups but we're on the boil with both techniques now,' said Billy. 'It has been outstanding to watch everyone's posts on the Camp Oven Facebook page each week and Linc is certain that he had a one-on-one with the Camp Oven Gods a few weeks ago. You've got to love Captain Morgan.'

Andy's Homemade Cooking Devices

North-west NSW handyman Andy O'Connell puts another 'r' in larrikin. He lives for his camp oven cooking and crafting his own equipment.

His backyard shed is decked out for the ultimate cook-off and boasts a series of different sized camp ovens and a homemade pizza oven and camp oven burner. His pizza oven is made up of a series of tyre rims stacked and welded on top of each other with a heat box attached on top with a door. Simply stoke the oven up underneath with wood and use the oven on top for a perfect pizza.

His camp oven cooker is unique. Centred around a keg in the middle which makes the coals, two plough discs are welded to each end with camp oven holders to regulate the heat. That's gold Andy.

Brad's Firepit

Brad Gallagher and his family live just outside of Gunnedah in North West NSW. At least once a week they join forces around their superbly crafted fire pit for a camp oven cook off.

Brad used around 40 heat-proof bricks at $70 each to manufacture his ring and concreted the base with a mix that consisted of more sand than rock. Four hanging points for camp ovens were placed around the ring for a cook-off to rival anybody's.

He has easy access to his wood pile metres from his coal pit and has spun more than one tall tale around the flames while enjoying 15–20 XXXX Gold beers (in his 20-year-old tin stubby holder) in a single session.

Donno's Diner

He calls it Donno's Diner ... and what a little beauty.

Craig Donaldson, a former Gunnedah larrikin now living in Belmont, Newcastle got hold of an old hot water system which cost him nothing.

After a weekend of beer-fuelled craftsmanship and a few welding rods, this is the creation he manufactured.

Strategically placed in his Man Cave, Donno's Diner is a Jack of all Trades and can smoke, roast, can be used as a spit or a pizza oven, or simply just build a fire in the base of it and warm yourself while smashing a rum and Coke.

Al's homemade Campfire Dagwood Dogs

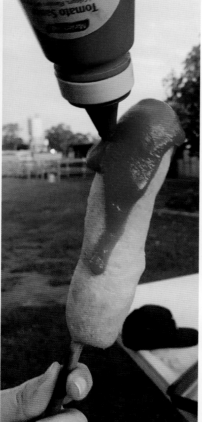

When it comes to crafting homemade Dagwood Dogs on the campfire, Gunnedah's Al Schillert is the undisputed king. A boiler-maker by trade, Al manufactured a steel base welded to a tube in the workshop which houses Crisco oil and two dagwood dogs at a time.

The batter comprises two cups of self-raising flour, one egg, salt and pepper and water, which he allows to stand for 30 minutes before going in for the dip. After threading the hot dog onto a water-soaked skewer, dip the 'dog' into the batter and place in the oil tube and brew until golden brown. Lash with copious amounts of tomato sauce to serve.

'I've cooked just about everything you can think of on spits and in the camp ovens but the Dagwood Dogs are the most popular with the kids by far,' said Al.

Jaffle Irons

If you want to take toasted sangas to the next level, start cooking with a jaffle iron, which you can find for between $25–$35 in any camping store. You can craft a toasted sandwich over flames, coals or on a gas burner, anywhere, anytime.

Make your sandwich with any filling you want but cheese is usually an essential ingredient. Who doesn't like melted cheese?

Butter the outside of both slices of bread and clamp the sandwich between the jaffle iron compart-ments. Trim off any excess bread crust otherwise it will burn and the sandwich will taste like charcoal.

Keep rotating the iron on heat, constantly opening and checking until you get a gold brown crust. Cook on a very low heat so filling cooks before bread burns.

Make sure you let sandwich cool down before digging in or you will end up with blistered lips.

My favourite jaffle iron comprises prawn, cheese, asparagus, onion and paprika. That's Gold.

History of The Great Aussie Jaffle Iron

According to *The Australian Food History Timeline*, the humble Jaffle Iron was designed and patented in Australia in 1949 by Dr Ernest Smithers of Bondi. Jaffles were touted as 'the latest cookery creation for all the family to enjoy'.

To get things going just make a thick sandwich, spray the insides of the jaffle iron with a bit of oil, clamp the sandwich shut in the iron and heat it over a flame.

The origins of the jaffle iron go back to Medieval times when they used wafer irons to make flat cakes.

The Belgian Waffle Iron evolved from the wafer iron no doubt provided inspiration for The Jaffle Iron.

Similar devices were available in America as early as the 1920s. In the USA they are called pie irons, pudgy pie irons or 'tonka toasters'.

Jaffle Queen Dessert Jaffles

2 slices of fruit bread per jaffle
Butter, softened (or other spread)
Jam of choice (strawberry used in these jaffles)

Filling for first jaffle:
Apple, sliced
Peaches, sliced, tinned or fresh
Sherry-soaked cranberries
Coconut
Cinnamon

Filling for second jaffle:
Banana, sliced
Rum-soaked raisins or sultanas
Chocolate chips
Cinnamon

Preheat the jaffle irons. Open up on a heat resistant surface and grease with oil spray or spread.

Butter the outside of one slice of fruit bread and press the buttered side down in the jaffle iron. Spread the inside of the bread with jam. Load the filling generously onto the bread. Spread jam on the other slice of fruit bread and place jam-side down over the filling. Butter the outside of the bread.

Close the jaffle lid carefully, making sure the top piece of bread stays in line with the bottom one. Trim off any overhanging bread crusts or they will burn.

Place the jaffle iron/s on hot coals or a gas ring and cook for a few minutes on each side. Carefully open the iron up and check if the jaffle is cooked, they should be sizzling and a beautiful golden colour. Enjoy with ice cream, yoghurt etc.

Building a Firepit in Your Backyard

Skye Rennick and Bryce Thompson

So this was a long-awaited weekend project for my partner, Bryce Thompson, and I. We started by clearing the area of loose debris and making sure the ground was level. Then we placed an old car tyre in the middle of where we wanted the pit. Then we placed the pavers/bricks corner-to-corner, fanning out, kind of like the sun. Then we placed the next round in an overlapping pattern until we had six layers of bricks all the way around (to make sure there is good airflow to the flames we recommend leaving small gaps in these levels).

We picked a point at the back of the pit where we wanted the point to be and then built up the bricks to the point. We used approximately 350–400 kiln-fired bricks (have to use these as others will not stand the heat). The bricks are actually cold to touch on the outside of the pit even when the flames are roaring but as an extra precaution, as it is a neighbour's fence, we have put cement sheeting behind the pit.

The pit is located in Wodonga just south of the NSW border. All in all this was such a fun project and has meant that an area that wasn't much use to us at all is now one of our focal points.

Wheelbarrow Cooking on Rainy Days

You have to be innovative when in lockdown!

Camp oven roast chicken for Sunday lunch, unexpected welcome storm means moving our transportable camp oven set-up under cover. All good.

This is our normal set-up for home cook-up when we can't travel and have a real fire. Love your work everyone. Great ideas.

Cheers,

Yvonne Geall

Biloela

TURBULENCE

Here's a tale of Billy Hayes from out near Alice Springs,
A wild young ringer who in his day had done some crazy things.
He'd jumped bulls over fences, raced a colt up Ayers Rock,
See, his legs weren't built for walking, they were made for riding stock.
A legend 'round the rodeos from Aileron to Broome,
An untried horse at 6am was saddle-broke by noon.
No form of equine foolery Bill wasn't game to try,
Only one thing ever spooked him – he was way too scared to fly.
'Ay, if I was meant to do it I'd have feathers and a beak,
'You take the plane there in a day. I'll drive and waste a week.
'I've been told they're safe as houses and mechanically they're sound,
'I don't see no rope or bridle so, ay, I'm sticking on the ground!'
But one day Billy got a phone call from his mate in Adelaide
Who'd got his girl in trouble so the wedding cards were played.
'Aw, Bill, I don't care how ya do it, ya can beg or steal or borra,
'But mate you've gotta take the plane, ay, 'cause the big day's on tomorra!'
Well, Billy cursed and spat it, said 'That dopey bloody coot,'
'He knows I'd jump on anything that's comin' out a chute.
'I've caught stallions that'd kill ya, caught bulls gone off their brain,
'Never thought there'd come the day I'd hafta catch a plane!'
He legged it to the airport, he thought 'Well this is it'.
The lady at the counter asked 'Where would you like to sit?'
He said 'Ahh, you know that black box thing they always seem to find,
'Well you can stick me right inside it if ya wouldn't bloody mind!'
The lady smiled politely and said 'Sir, I'll just take your bag'.
He said 'I don't bloody think so and by the way it's called a swag'.
Bill was sweating buckets when they finally cleared the strip,
He had his seatbelt on that tight he was bleeding from the hip
But when they levelled out he stopped shaking at the knees,
Looked around, relaxed and thought 'This flyin' game's a breeze'.
He clipped his belt undone, stretched out in his seat,
Well, he couldn't stretch that far because his swag was at his feet.
Then the captain crackled something, Bill asked a hostess what was said,
'Sir, you'd better buckle up there's some turbulence ahead'.
He said 'Turbulence, what's that?' 'Sir it's pockets caused by heat
'And when it gets severe it can throw you from your seat.'
He said 'Throw me, I'll be buggered', he pushed his seat right back,
Wrapped his legs around his swag and stuck his left hand through the strap,
He jammed down his Akubra, he was ready now to ride
Then things got pretty bumpy and Billy yelled 'OUTSIDE!'
The plane she dropped a thousand feet, rose up five hundred more,
When his head near hit the ceiling he gave a mighty roar,
'I've rode all through the Territ'ry and never come unstuck,
'So give me all you've got big bird and buck you bastard buck!'
And while the passengers were screaming in fear of certain death
Billy whooped and hollered 'til he near ran out of breath.

You would've thought that canvas swag was welded to his ass
And before the ringer knew it he'd bucked up to business class!
There seemed no way to tame this creature, it had ten gears and reverse,
That didn't worry Billy, he just bucked on through to first!
He'd done somersaults with twists on this mongrel mount from hell,
He yelled out to the pilot *'For Christ's sake, ring the bell!'*
Poor old Bill was bleeding from the bugle, he had cuts above both eyes,
If you weren't there on the spot you prob'ly think I'm telling lies.

He'd been upside down, inside out, done flips and triple spins,
You might've seen some great rides in your time but hands down Billy wins.
The flight returned to normal, Bill was flat out on the deck,
Still stuck to his swag but geez, he looked a bloody wreck.
He pulled himself together, stood up and raised his hat,
He said *'I've had some tough trips in my time but never one like that.*
'An eight-second spin in Alice proves you're made of sturdy stuff,
'I was on there near a minute and I reckon that's enough.'
Well the first class folk were dumbstruck at this crazy ringer's feat
But Bill just grabbed a Crownie and he walked back to his seat.
Now years have passed and Bill's long give the bucking game away,
Too many breaks and dusty miles for far too little pay,
Now planes are not a problem, in fact he'd rather fly than ride
And when you talk about his maiden voyage his chest puffs out with pride.
'You can talk about your Rocky Neds and that old Chainsaw bloke,
'I'd ride 'em both without a rope and roll a bloody smoke.
'There's cowboys 'round who think they're hot, well they ain't tasted heat
''Til they've ridden time on Turbulence at 30,000 feet!'

Murray Hartin

CHILLI RING-BURNERS, Indian and Italian

Butter Chicken

Marinade

1kg boneless skinless chicken thighs, cut into pieces

½ cup plain yoghurt

1½ tbsp minced garlic

1 tbsp finely grated ginger

2 tbsp Garam Masala

1 tsp turmeric

1 tsp ground cumin

1 tsp red chilli powder

1 tsp salt

Sauce

1 tsp butter

2 tbsp olive oil

1 large brown onion, chopped

1½ tbsp minced garlic

1 tsp ground coriander

1½ tsp ground cumin

1½ tsp Garam Masala

400g can crushed tomatoes

1 tsp red chilli (adjust to your taste)

1½ tsp salt

1 cup thick cream

1 tbsp sugar

In a bowl combine the chicken with the marinade ingredients and marinate for about 1 hour or overnight.

Heat oil in a camp oven and add the marinated chicken in batches to brown on each side for 3 minutes then place in a separate bowl for later.

Melt the butter with the oil and fry the onion. Scrape up any brown bits from the bottom of the camp oven. Add the garlic and cook for 1 minute until fragrant. Add the coriander, cumin and Garam Masala, let cook for 20 minutes, stirring occasionally.

Add the crushed tomatoes, chilli powder and salt, let simmer for about 10–15 minutes, stirring occasionally until the sauce thickens.

Remove from the heat and blend with a stick blender until smooth, you can add water to help blend if you need to. Stir in the cream and sugar then add the chicken pieces and juices back in and cook for another 8–10 minutes until the chicken is cooked through and the sauce is thick and bubbling.

Garnish with chopped coriander and serve with boiled rice and fresh homemade garlic naan bread.

Easy Naan Bread

260g self-raising flour
1 tsp baking powder
1 tsp sugar
Pinch of salt
1 cup plain yoghurt
2 tsp olive oil
Splash of milk
Garlic, finely sliced
Nigella seeds

In a large bowl combine the self-raising flour, baking powder, sugar and salt. Make a well in the centre of the mixture and add the yoghurt, olive oil and a splash of milk. Mix together to form a dough, add another splash of milk if it's too dry. Knead on a lightly floured board, roll out into naan size pieces and top with garlic and nigella seeds. Cook in the camp oven and brush with melted butter when cooked.

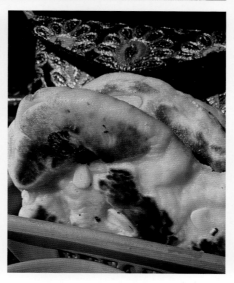

Chilli Con Carne

1 tbsp olive oil

3 garlic cloves, minced

1 brown onion, diced

Beef mince

4 tbsp tomato paste

1 can crushed tomatoes

2 beef stock cubes

1½ tsp sugar

1½ cups water

Salt and pepper

1 can 4 bean mix or red kidney beans

Chilli spice mix

1 tsp cayenne pepper or fresh chilli to taste

4 tsp paprika powder

5 tsp cumin power

2 tsp onion power

2 tsp oregano

To serve

Corn chips

Sour cream

Grated cheese

Fresh salsa

Coriander

Heat the oil in a camp oven on medium heat, add the garlic and onion and cook for 1 minute.

Add the beef and cook on high heat, breaking up the mince as you go, cook until browned.

Add all remaining ingredients and cook on low heat with the lid on for 1½–2 hours covered, bubbling gently. Add extra salt and pepper to serve.

Chilli Time Tacos

2kg beef mince

2 packets taco seasoning mix

1–2 chillis (depending on how hot you like it)

Water

Lettuce

Tomatoes

Avocados

Cheese

Sour Cream

Cucumber

Place the camp oven on top of coals to heat.

Brown the mince, add the taco seasoning mix and chilli with enough water to mix it all together and let it simmer for however long you want it to simmer for.

While it's simmering away, get together all your other ingredients and dice it all up.

When you are ready to serve, stack your taco shells, taco boats or wraps with your toppings. Enjoy!

Spaghetti Bolognese

1.5kg beef mince

1 can tomatoes

About 5 cocktail tomatoes
squashed in your hand

A good splash of Dolmio sauce

Water

Basil

Garlic

Zested lemon

Chilli

Bay leaves

Tomato paste

Salt and pepper

Splash of red wine

Brown the mince in the camp
oven then throw everything in.
Cook the pasta and enjoy!

Sausage and Beans Chilli Veg

This one's an easy one. Use a sausage of your choice, we used pork! Add chorizo, beans, beans and more beans (of your choice). Some veg, celery, capsicum, corn... whatever you like! Don't forget the chilli for a bit of bite.

Just brown the sausages then cook off the vegies and add a few cans of beans (Heinz Beanz Creations Spanish style are recommended). Let it slowly cook in the camp oven. Delicious with some crusty bread and butter.

The Ring-Burner Mexican Pizza

(Nailed in a Camp Oven on a Butane Burner.)

ENTER AT YOUR OWN RISK.
Medium pizza base from supermarket or make your own
Garlic and herb tomato pizza base sauce
Chilli paste
Grated cheese
1 packet of pepperoni circles
1 capsicum (red looks best), diced
1 fresh Jalapeno pepper, diced
1 onion, diced
Mushrooms, diced
1 large red chilli, sliced

Lay your pizza base on a cutting board, smear with garlic and herb tomato paste and a suggestion of chilli paste to taste.

Cover the base with grated cheese and place the pepperoni circles over the top in a smart pattern. Add the capsicum, jalapeno, onion mushrooms and more chilli and sprinkle all over the pizza to taste.

The last step is to sparingly cover the whole pizza with more grated cheese. Season with pepper and you are ready to head to the camp oven.

Pre-heat the camp oven for 5 minutes with the lid on. I place two trivets in the oven to get the pizza well off the hot base and then a small sheet of baking paper on top of the trivet lightly sprayed with canola oil. Place the pizza in the oven, put the lid on, turn the heat down and PRAY.

Try to wait 7–8 minutes before lifting the lid and checking that the base is not over cooking. Repeat until the toppings are cooked but continually watch the base, you don't want it black. Serve with damper or garlic bread and a cold stubby of VB.

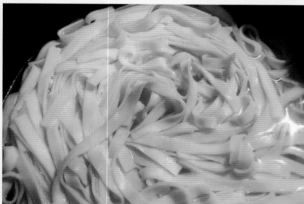

Serves 6

1 tbsp butter

1 large brown onion, finely diced

2 tbsp minced garlic or 4 cloves chopped

250g mushrooms, sliced

Salt and pepper

1kg chicken thighs, diced into bite-sized bits

4 full rashers of bacon, chopped

600ml thickened cream

125g packet of grated Parmesan cheese

2 spring onions, diced

2 packets of fresh egg fettuccine (or a large packet of dried)

Heat up the camp oven, add the butter and brown the onions with garlic before adding the mushrooms and seasoning with salt and pepper. Cook lightly for 5 minutes then add the chicken and cook for another 10 minutes (or until there is no pinkness). Add diced bacon and fry off for another couple of minutes.

Add the cream and stir in half of the packet of Parmesan cheese then add the shallots (white part only). Cook on very low heat for half an hour with the lid off the camp oven to reduce the cream to a thick sauce.

Serve with fresh egg fettuccine and buttered sourdough. Sprinkle the remaining Parmesan cheese over the top before serving and garnish with chopped shallots (green part). A beautiful camp oven feed everyone will enjoy, especially the kids.

Note: After the chicken is cooked if the camp oven mix is too dry, add ½ cup of chicken stock or pasta water.

Angry Kransky Chilli Dog

WARNING: Enter at Own Risk, this is spicy hot!
Not recommended for kids.

2 chilli and cheese kranskys
2 sheets of puff pastry
4 hot chorizo salami rings
4 slices of cheese or 1 cup grated cheese
Diced fresh chillies to taste
Crushed chilli paste
2 jalapenos
1 onion, diced
Pepper
Milk
1 tub Greek yoghurt

Cook the kranskys in the camp oven for 6–8 minutes, continually turning. Remove from the oven and set aside to cool.

Lay out one sheet of puff pastry and place the kransky wrapped in salami rings at the bottom end. Moving towards the centre of sheet, tightly lay in the cheese, fresh chillies, chilli paste, jalapenos, onion and season with pepper.

Carefully wrap and roll in the pastry, folding each end. Brush the pastry all over with milk and place in the camp oven on a trivet lined with baking paper. Cook on a low heat with the lid slightly lifted with a knife so steam can escape. Continually check and turn the pastry until golden brown. Serve with a generous amount of yoghurt which will counteract the sensational eye-watering, head tingling heat. Good luck!

Note: If you do not use a trivet you will likely burn the pastry before it has cooked through. The reason you want the lid slightly risen is to stop the Chilli Dog from steaming and turning to mush.

Beef Vinda-Gottagotothe-Loo

Traditionally one of the hottest Indian style dishes but you can make it as hot or as mild as you want. These are the basic instructions to crafting a Beef Vindaloo in your trusty camp oven.

¼ cup white vinegar
¼ cup garlic paste
¼ cup ginger paste
2 tbsp plain yoghurt
1 tbsp paprika (mild) or 1 tbsp cayenne pepper
1 tbsp salt
1 tbsp black ground pepper
1kg beef chuck steak, cut into chunks
Vegetable oil
2 brown onions, chopped
2 tomatoes
1 large red chilli, diced
1 cup water
Basmati rice

Mix the vinegar, garlic and ginger pastes, yoghurt, paprika or cayenne pepper, salt and black pepper in a mixing bowl and add the beef cubes, coating all the meat thoroughly. Cover and place in the fridge for 2 hours before cooking. If you can, overnight will ensure the meat is well marinated.

Heat oil in the camp oven and soften the onions (about 5 minutes) before adding the seasoned beef cubes. Cook until the meat browns (about 10 minutes) and then stir in the chopped tomatoes. Add the diced chilli and cook for a further 5 minutes.

Pour in the water and bring to the simmer. Cook on a very low heat until the meat is tender, continually stirring throughout (about 2 hours should do the job).

Serve on a bed of basmati rice with a side of crusty bread or naan and keep a toilet within running distance on completion of the meal.

Remember you can add or remove whatever you want from this dish and make it as hot as you want. Choosing cayenne pepper with diced red chillies will ensure plenty of heat while paprika will produce a much milder brew.

THE SHOPPING BAGS FIASCO

It's a finite world we live in,
Of that there's little doubt,
The ice caps and the ozone
And the trees are running out.

I recycle when I can
But I'm being driven mad
By those environmental *'Save the Planet'*
BRIGHT GREEN SHOPPING BAGS!!

Don't pretend you haven't bought 'em,
They bloody got me too,
The voice of guilt booms through the aisles
When you're trying to buy some food.

A constant message warns you
'Plastic kills' and *'It's your choice'*,
So you buy the bright green shopping bags
Just to stop the voice.

But now the herbal groovy checkout chick
Who used to snarl and look away
Fills your new bags with a smile
And says *'Have a lovely day'*.

And the new bags hold much more
So it's not just conservation,
Plus they're easy on the grip
And don't cut your circulation

So, on the journey to your vehicle,
The usual half a mile,
You think the bags are pretty cool
And you crack a little smile.

You get home feeling fairly smug,
Pack the food away,
Stick the new bags in the cupboard
And that's where they bloody stay!

You never take them to the shops!
You don't remember 'til you're there!
So you're back to using plastic
And the checkout chick just glares.

So you buy more bright green shopping bags
To get her back on side
And they end up in the cupboard
Where the other mongrels died!

Well, they're not dead, they're just asleep,
I mean nitro glycerin
Couldn't kill these bags,
They're made of poly-propylene.

Environmentally friendly?!
They'd survive a nuclear blast,
We're talking heavy-duty gear
That makes plastic look like grass.

So you stick some in your car,
You won't forget them now,
Well of course you bloody do,
You just can't work out how.

It doesn't matter where you put them,
In the boot or in the front,
You could hang them 'round your neck,
You'll still only use them once!

They keep selling me these bags
And they know I've got a stack,
In the car, in the cupboard,
Don't forget the granny flat.

I want to do the right thing
So I keep on buying more
Just because that I forget
To bring the ones I bought before.

Meanwhile, the price of poly-propylene
Is going through the roof,
Well, I don't know that for sure,
I haven't got much proof.

But someone's making money
And it sure as hell ain't me,
I've got a thousand bright green shopping bags
And they cost three bucks a piece!

So while I'd love to save the planet
And the green bags are fantastic,
My accountant said, to save my house,
I have to stick to plastic.

Murray Hartin

PIZZA AND DAMPER

Beetroot and Chocolate Damper

2 cups self-raising flour
2 tbsp cocoa powder
80g butter
½ cup sugar
Handful of chocolate chips
1–3 tbsp milk
1 egg
1 cup cooked and blended beetroot
Flaked almonds to decorate

Place the flour in a large bowl and mix in the cocoa powder. Add the cold cubed butter to the flour mixture and use your fingertips to rub the butter in until the mixture resembles fine breadcrumbs.

In a small bowl mix together the sugar, chocolate chips, milk, egg and beetroot. Add that to the flour mixture and use a round bladed knife in a cutting motion to mix together.

Turn out onto a floured board and knead a small amount.

Line a camp oven with baking paper and place the damper inside, you can cut a cross on the top and sprinkle with flaked almonds if you wish. I cooked mine on hot coals top and bottom for 30 minutes, just a guide, cooking times can vary so just keep a close eye on it!

Enjoy my creation, made with love!

Camp Oven Brekky Omelettes

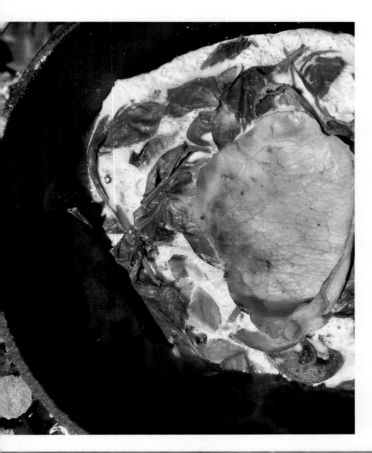

Serves 4 (but add whatever you like)

6 short cut bacon rashers
1 tbsp oil
8 eggs
½ cup milk
½ cup grated cheese
Handful of mushrooms
10 cherry tomatoes cut in half or 2 regular tomatoes
Handful of baby spinach leaves
Salt and pepper

Cook the bacon with oil in the camp oven. While the bacon is cooking, crack the eggs into another camp oven and whisk lightly, add the milk and stir through. Add the rest of the ingredients. Cut up the bacon and add to the omelette, saving one piece to place on top. Add salt and pepper to taste. Cook for about 20 minutes.

Pizza Night: Prawn, Meat Lovers, Supreme, Chicken and Bacon

Prawn Pizza

Dolmio sauce

Cheese

Garlic

Chilli

Prawns

Rocket

Lemon

Spread the pizza base with sauce then cheese, garlic, chilli and then top with prawns. When the pizza is cooked top with some rocket and a squeeze of lemon. Bake till brown on top... yummo!

Meat Lovers

BBQ sauce

Cheese

Pepperoni

Chorizo

Cooked Sausage

Bacon

Onion

Mushrooms

Shallots

Spread the pizza base with BBQ sauce then top with some cheese. Top with the rest of the ingredients and then cook till brown on top.

Supreme

Whatever sauce you want on the bottom

Whatever you have in the fridge on the top

Cheese

Spread the base with the sauce then add whatever you have in the fridge and top with some cheese... perfect!

Chicken and Bacon

BBQ sauce

Bacon

Chicken

Cheese

Spread the base with sauce, top with bacon, chicken and then cheese. Cook until brown.

Damper

Mix 4 cups of self-raising flour with enough water just to combine, it's not a wet mixture and you don't need to knead it. Just work it into a shape that you want. That's about it. When it's ready put golden syrup over it or honey. Tip: Cook on slow heat on a trivet until the damper starts to turn golden brown.

Pizza See-food And Eat It

Seafood marinara
Medium pizza base (store-bought or make your own)
Garlic and herb tomato pizza base sauce
Grated cheese
Black pepper

Fry off the seafood marinara in a pan for 5–6 minutes then set aside. Place your pizza base on a cutting board and smear with garlic and herb tomato paste.

Cover the base with grated cheese, scatter the marinara over the top and season with black pepper. The last step is to sparingly cover the pizza with more grated cheese.

Pre-heat the camp oven for 5 minutes with the lid on. I place two trivets in the oven to get the pizza well off the hot base and then place a small sheet of baking paper lightly sprayed with oil on top of the trivet. Place the pizza in the oven and cook on low heat for 10–12 minutes, constantly checking that the base is not burning. Serve with damper or garlic bread.

Perfect Pull-Apart Pizza

Laucke Pizza dough mix or store-bought pizza dough
¼ cup olive oil
1 small onion, chopped
2 tbsp Italian herbs
½ tsp garlic powder
1 small green capsicum, diced
Salami, diced
Ham, diced
1 cup tasty cheese
2 cups mozzarella cheese

Follow the directions on the pizza mix packet. When the dough has been kneaded and rested, halve the dough. Roll into a cylinder shapes, lightly dust with flour then wrap in plastic wrap and chill in the fridge for about 1 hour. Remove from the fridge and take out of the plastic. Slice into 2cm slices then cut each slice in quarters. Place in large mixing bowl and add the olive oil to coat the dough. Add all remaining ingredients and gently mix together. Line a tin with baking paper and add the dough and ingredients. Cook for about 30 minutes and make sure your coals are on top and bottom.

Note: The camp oven must be preheated to a hot temperature before cooking the pizza.

Double Smoked Ham Pizza

2 tbsp olive oil

150g small field mushrooms, finely sliced

2 tbsp balsamic vinegar

2 tbsp caster sugar

Coarse semolina for dusting

1 quantity pizza dough

½ quantity basic pizza sauce

2 tbsp flatleaf parsley, chopped

75g grated mozzarella cheese

70g double-smoked ham, torn into pieces

30g Taleggio cheese

Heat the olive oil in a heavy based frying pan over high heat, add the mushrooms and cook for 4–5 minutes or until golden. Remove from the heat to taste.

Meanwhile, put the balsamic vinegar and sugar in a small saucepan and simmer over low heat until reduced by two-thirds. Remove from the heat and set aside.

Place the pizza stone or heavy-based oven tray in the oven and preheat to 250°C. Lightly dust your workbench with semolina then roll out the dough into a 30cm round, place on a pizza tray and prick all over with a fork.

Spread the pizza sauce over the base then scatter with parsley, mozzarella, mushrooms and ham in that order. Tear the Taleggio into small pieces and scatter over the top then place the tray on the preheated stone or tray and bake for 5–6 minutes or until the base is golden and crisp. Remove from the oven, drizzle with the reduced balsamic vinegar and serve.

Pescatore Pizza

2 tbsp olive oil

10 black mussels

1 river calamari, cleaned and cut into 5mm thick rings, tentacles reserved

10 raw small prawns, peeled and deveined

60g skinless firm white fish fillet, cut into 1cm pieces

100g baby octopus, cleaned and cut into 2cm pieces

2 tbsp flatleaf parsley, chopped

½ quantity basic pizza sauce

Coarse semolina for dusting

1 quantity pizza dough

75g grated mozzarella cheese

Lemon wedges to serve

Heat 1 tbsp of the olive oil in a large heavy-based frying pan and add the mussels, cover and shake the pan over high heat for 3 minutes or just until the shells open. Pour into a colander over a bowl (reserving the juices) and, when cool enough to handle, remove the meat from the shells. Discard any unopened mussels.

Return the pan to the heat, add the remaining oil then add the calamari rings and tentacles, prawns, fish and octopus and toss over high heat for 2 minutes or until nearly cooked through. Add the parsley and season to taste then pour the seafood into a colander placed over a bowl and return the pan to the heat. Add the pizza sauce and any juices from the seafood (including the mussel juice) and simmer over low heat for 6 minutes or until slightly thickened.

Place a pizza stone or heavy based oven tray in the oven and pre-heat to 250°C. Lightly dust your workbench with semolina then roll out the dough into a 30cm round, place on a pizza tray and prick all over with a fork. Place on the preheated stone or tray and bake for 5–6 minutes or until the base is golden and crisp. Serve with lemon wedges for squeezing over.

Puttanesco Pizza

Coarse semolina for dusting
1 quantity pizza dough
½ quantity basic pizza sauce
180g cherry tomatoes, thinly sliced
1 tbsp capers
3 tbsp pitted black or green olives
4 anchovy fillets
1 tbsp flatleaf parsley, chopped
1 tbsp garlic confit, finely chopped
75g grated mozzarella cheese

Place a pizza stone or heavy-based oven tray in the oven and pre-heat to 250°C. Lightly dust your workbench with semolina then roll out the dough into a 30cm round, place on a pizza tray and prick all over with a fork. Spread the base with the pizza sauce then scatter with the remaining ingredients and season to taste. Place on the pre-heated stone or tray and bake for 5–6 minutes or until the base is golden and crisp.

Smoked Trout Calzone

8 local black mussels, cleaned
2 fresh red bird's eye chillies, seeded and finely chopped
1 anchovy fillet
30g broccolini, blanched and finely chopped
100g skinless smoked rainbow trout, bones removed and flesh flaked
50g provolone picante cheese
40g buffalo mozzarella cheese, torn
Coarse semolina for dusting
1 quantity pizza dough

Heat a small heavy-based saucepan over medium-high heat until very hot, add the mussels, cover and shake for 3 minutes or just until the shells open. Pour the mussels into a colander placed over a bowl, remove the meat and discard the shells. Return the mussel cooking liquid to the pan, add the chillies, anchovy, broccolini and trout and stir over low heat for 5 minutes or until fragrant and well combined. Remove from the heat then fold in the provolone and season to taste.

Place a pizza stone or heavy based oven tray in the oven and preheat to 190°C.

Lightly dust your workbench with semolina then roll out the dough into a 30cm round and place on a pizza tray. Spread the mixture over one side of the base, sprinkle with the mozzarella then fold the other side over the filling and pinch the edges together to prevent any juices escaping. Place on the preheated stone or tray and bake for 8–10 minutes or until crisp and golden.

Pear Dumplings

For the pears

2 bottles dry white wine

¼ cup freshly squeezed lemon juice, plus the peel of 2 lemons

2 cups granulated sugar

2 cinnamon sticks

1 vanilla bean, halved and seeded

5 pears

For the crust

Pate Briscee, rolled to 1/8 inch, chilled

For finishing

½ cup granulated sugar

4 tsp ground cinnamon

4 tbsp cold unsalted butter, cut into small pieces

1 egg, beaten with 2 tsp of water for glaze

Fine sanding sugar (optional)

Poach the pears by combining the white wine, lemon juice and peel, granulated sugar, cinnamon sticks and vanilla bean and seeds in medium saucepan over high heat. Bring to the boil and cook for 5 minutes. Add the pears, lowering the heat, and cook for 20–30 minutes, until the pears are tender. If necessary turn the pears very gently by rotating the stems with your fingertips so that they cook evenly.

Remove the pears to a bowl, bring the poaching liquid to a rapid boil and reduce by half.

Pour the syrup over the pears and refrigerate, covered, for at least 6 hours, preferably overnight.

Assemble the dumplings. Roll out the pastry to a thickness of no more than 1/8 inch. Using a sharp knife or pastry wheel, cut the dough into triangles (using the pear as a guide for the size). Cut as many leaf shapes as possible from the pastry scraps and use the back of a paring knife to make the vein markings.

Preheat the oven to 400°C. Mix the sugar and cinnamon in a small bowl and set aside. Remove the pears from the poaching syrup and pat dry. Reduce the syrup to about 1 cup for serving. Using a Parisian scoop, core each piece of fruit carefully, starting from the bottom to within ¾ inch of the top; take care to leave the stem intact. Fill each fruit with some of the cinnamon/sugar mixture (and sultanas) and dot with butter.

Invert each pear onto the centre of the triangle of pastry. Lightly brush the edges of dough with the egg wash. Bring the edges of the pastry together and pinch to seal.

Garnish the dumplings as desired by pasting the leaves on with egg wash. Lightly brush each dumpling with the egg wash and, if desired, sprinkle with sanding sugar. Place the dumplings on a parchment lined baking sheet and chill until ready to bake.

Cover the stems with a small piece of foil. Bake in the upper third of the oven for 30 minutes. Transfer to wire rack and cool slightly, about 15–20 minutes. Spoon a 1–2 tbsp of reduced syrup around the base of each pear. Serve warm.

Bolognese Pide/Pizza

Dough

2 cups plain flour

1 tsp salt

1 tsp instant yeast

2 tbsp olive oil

1 tbsp honey

Filling

250g beef mince

1 onion

1 garlic clove

1 large tomato (or tinned tomato)

2 tbsp tomato paste

Mixed herbs

1 cup grated mozzarella cheese (or any grated cheese)

½ cup grated parmesan

Oil

Note: Add your own Bolognese herbs and spices. Substitute Bolognese for tuna mornay, spinach and feta or any leftovers you like.

Dough

Mix the flour, salt and yeast in a bowl, making a well in the centre. Pour in the oil and honey with ¾ cup of tepid water. Bring together to form a soft dough, add a little extra water if the dough feels too dry. Knead for about 5 minutes on a lightly floured surface. Put the dough in an oiled bowl and cover with a cloth for 2 hours. When the dough has doubled in size, punch the air out and roll out to the size of your camp oven plus a little more to pull up the sides.

Filling

Fry off the mince, onion, garlic and tomato. Add the tomato paste and herbs. Spoon the cooled mixture onto the pizza base in the camp oven, top with the mixed cheeses. Pull the sides around the mixture and paint with olive oil. Your pide is ready to cook.

Curry Prawn Pizza and Ham Bruschetta Pizza

Curry Prawn Pizza

Make and roll out the pizza base in the camp oven (we used Laucke pizza/focaccia flour mix) and top with tomato paste. Cook the prawns in some curry powder for a few minutes then place them on top of the pizza. Sprinkle with feta, cherry tomatoes and ham and top with mozzarella cheese. Place the camp oven on hot coals and put coals on top of the oven too. Cook for 15–20 minutes. Enjoy with a beer or three!

Ham Bruschetta Pizza

Make and roll out the pizza base in the camp oven and top with tomato paste. Sprinkle chopped cherry tomatoes, red onion, diced ham, feta and basil leaves over the pizza and top with mozzarella cheese. Place the camp oven on hot coals and put coals on top of the oven too. Cook for 15–20 minutes.

Carefully use a spatula to remove the pizzas from the camp ovens and put on a baking tray so you can cut them easily.

THE FARMER – THE PEARL OF THEM ALL

Australia is chock-full of champions
And history will keep safe their names
We share moments of proud men and women
Who have climbed to the top of their game,
They provide us with great inspiration
But if I may make a very big call
If the aim is to recognise champions
I think The Farmer's the Pearl of Them All.

See the tough game he's in never ends
And the playing field's often quite rough
You need wet stuff to fill up the rain gauge
Talent and hope aren't enough
Resilience plays a huge factor
Without it the greatest may fall
And our champion has got it in spades
The Farmer, The Pearl of Them All

Plus courage to push through the hard times
You need it to last on the land
While the Rain Gods can smile on you sweetly
Control can still slip from your hands
Too much is as bad as too little
A flood rocks him right to the core
But he mops up and continues the battle
The Farmer, The Pearl of Them All

Sometimes there are knee-jerk reactions
From those who are desperate for votes
Who pretend to be well-versed in matters
But wouldn't know chick peas from oats
While he tries to make sense of this madness
That again puts his back to the wall
Each day he heads out to the paddock
The Farmer, The Pearl of Them All

Look, it's not all rotten luck and bad seasons
When the planets align life is sweet
He knows when he gets a fair go
His produce is real hard to beat
He'll knock the froth off a couple of cold ones
And most likely have a few more
To celebrate the life he has chosen
The Farmer – The Pearl of Them All

So next time the talk turns to heroes
A subject of much great debate
And you discuss who befits such a title
Spare a thought for our battling mate
In the history of all things Australian
He has well-earned the right to walk tall
So please raise a glass to our champion
The Farmer – The Pearl of Them All.

Inspired by Will Ogilvie's classic poem
'The Pearl of Them All'. Murray Hartin

SOUP KITCHEN

Thai Curried Pumpkin Soup

1 tbsp olive oil

1 brown onion, diced

3 garlic cloves, minced

2 tbsp red curry paste

1sp ground cumin

1 tsp ground ginger

½ tsp sea salt

½ Jarrah pumpkin, diced

1 butternut pumpkin, diced

3 cups chicken stock

1 can coconut milk

Heat the oil in the camp oven, add the onion and sauté for 5 minutes. Add the garlic, red curry paste, cumin, ginger and salt and cook for another 2 minutes. Add the pumpkin, chicken stock and coconut milk and simmer until the pumpkin is cooked through. Use a stick blender to purée the soup until smooth.

and Spinach Damper

2 cups self-raising flour
3 tbsp butter
1 egg
1–3 tbsp reduced fat milk
1 cup pumpkin mash
Handful of fresh basil
1 red roasted capsicum, skin removed, roughly chopped
Handful of baby spinach, finely chopped

Sift the flour in a large bowl. Rub the butter into the flour with your fingertips until it looks like breadcrumbs. In a separate bowl, add the egg and milk to the pumpkin mash, stir until well combined. Add the pumpkin mixture, basil, roasted capsicum and spinach to the flour and mix with a round bladed knife to combine. Turn the dough out onto a lightly floured work bench and knead until just smooth. Shape into a round disc.

Cook on baking paper in the camp oven for about 30 minutes or until the dough sounds hollow when tapped. Keep a close eye on it. Serve warm or cold with butter.

Creamy Tuscan Chicken Soup

2 onions, chopped

4 sticks celery, chopped

1.5kg chicken thighs, chopped

4 gloves garlic, crushed

Chilli flakes (optional)

2 cans drained and rinsed cannellini beans

½ cup sun-dried tomatoes, chopped

1L chicken stock

¼ cup cream

Baby spinach leaves

Sauté the onion and celery in a bit of oil then remove from the camp oven. Brown the chicken pieces then add all other ingredients except the cream and spinach and cook on slow heat for approximately 1 hour. When cooked, remove from the fire and stir in the cream. Add the baby spinach to a bowl and ladle the soup on top. Serve with damper or sourdough bread.

Lamb and Barley Soup

G'day fellow cough dodgers here's what I knocked up over the weekend in the old cast iron under the Kelvin range sunset. I was as full as a seaside outhouse on a bank holiday after a bowl of this.

Selection of soup vegetables (onion, carrot, celery, potato etc)
Whatever lamb you've got on hand (I used 4 shanks and a pack of lamb offcuts)
A pack of beef stock
Couple of bacon bones
Half a pack of dry soup mix
Water

I cooked this over two days. Dice up the soup vegetables, add the lamb (trimmed of as much fat as possible), beef stock, bacon bones, dry soup mix and about 4 cups of water. Cook over low heat for 4–5 hours. Allow to cool overnight. Skim off as much fat as possible. Cook over low heat again for another 3–4 hours till the lamb is falling off the bone. Serve with a nice crusty bread.

Chicken, Leek, Broccolini, Lentil and Spinach Soup

Oil

2 leeks, sliced

3 tsp fresh thyme leaves

3 celery stalks, sliced

1.7L water

3 x 28g chicken stock pots

600g chicken breasts

1 bunch Broccolini, cut into bite-sized pieces

400g can lentils

160g baby spinach leaves

Salt and pepper

Heat the oil then add the leeks, thyme and celery to the camp oven and cook until soft. Add water and stock pots then bring to a simmer. Poach the chicken breast in the soup for about 12–15 minutes until just cooked through. Remove the chicken and set aside to cool. Add the broccolini, stir though the lentils and spinach to warm. Remove from the heat and add salt and pepper. Shred the chicken breast and stir through the soup.

Prawn and Chorizo Gumbo

500g smoked sausage
½ cup vegetable oil
¾ cup plain flour
1 large brown onion, chopped
2 cups celery, chopped
1 green capsicum, chopped
1 red capsicum, chopped
1 tbsp minced fresh garlic (about 4 cloves)
1 jalapeño, minced
4 cups chicken broth
2 tbsp fresh thyme, chopped
1 tsp salt
½ tsp ground black pepper
4 bay leaves
1 can fire-roasted tomatoes, undrained
1kg medium fresh peeled prawns
1 tsp Creole seasoning
Cooked rice to serve
Sliced green onion to garnish

In a cast iron skillet or camp oven, cook the sausage over medium heat, stirring occasionally until browned, approximately 7 minutes. Remove the sausage from the skillet and set aside.

Add oil to the camp oven. Add flour, stirring until smooth. Cook, stirring constantly with a wooden spoon, until the mixture is a deep caramel colour, approximately 30 minutes. Add the onion, celery, capsicum, garlic and jalapeño. Cook, stirring constantly, until softened, approximately 5 minutes.

Gradually stir in the broth and bring to the boil then reduce heat to medium-low. Simmer, stirring constantly, until the mixture is smooth and has thickened, approximately 2 minutes. Add sausage, 1 tbsp thyme, salt, pepper, bay leaves and tomato.

Cover and cook on low for 3 hours. Add prawns, Creole seasoning and the remaining 1 tbsp of thyme. Cover and cook until the prawns are pink and firm, approximately 30 minutes, stirring twice. Discard bay leaves. Serve over rice. Garnish with green onion if desired.

Oxtail Soup

Oxtails are beef tails and they make the most delicious soup. While some people hesitate at the idea of eating a cow's tail, it is definitely a recipe to try. The soup does need a lot of time to simmer (perfect for the camp oven on low heat) because of the fatty meat but requires little work.

1kg oxtail
½ cup plain flour
2 tbsp cooking oil
2L water
2 tbsp tomato paste
250ml beef stock
2 medium onions, peeled and minced
2 medium carrots, peeled and diced
3 garlic cloves
½ tsp thyme
1 bay leaf
2 tsp salt
¼ tsp freshly ground pepper
2 sprigs fresh parsley

It doesn't get much easier than this. Coat the oxtail pieces in flour and lightly fry in the camp oven with a splash of oil for 5 minutes. Drain the excess oil and add the water, tomato paste, beef stock, chopped vegetables and garlic, thyme and bay leaves, and salt and pepper to taste. Cook on a low heat for two hours constantly stirring.

This is the sort of soup you can add anything to and it will taste sensational. These are just the basics to make sure you kick off on the right track with plenty of flavour. Serve with crusty bread and fresh parsley on top.

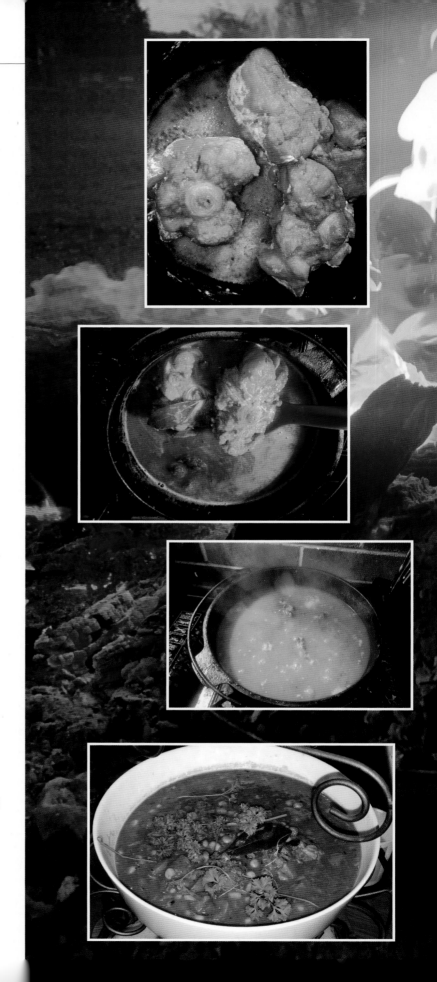

Pea And Ham Soup

2 carrots, peeled
2 celery sticks
1 brown onion
290g (1 1/3 cups) green split peas
3 garlic cloves, crushed
1 ham bone
700g (or more) bacon hocks
1.5L (or enough to cover all) cold water
Salt and freshly ground black pepper
Crusty bread or damper to serve

Chop up the carrots, celery and onion. Rinse the split peas under cold running water until the water is clear then drain. Add the split peas, carrot, celery, onion, garlic, ham bone and bacon hocks and water to the camp oven or slow cooker. Season with salt and pepper. Cook for 2–2½ hours always checking to monitor the heat and to give it a stir, or until the ham hocks are tender and the meat is falling away from the bones. If cooking in a slow cooker, cook for 6 hours on low heat. Remove the ham hocks from the pan. Remove the meat from the bones. Coarsely chop the meat and then add it back to the soup. Serve with damper or crusty bread.

Damper

3 cups (450g) self-raising flour
Pinch of salt
80g butter, chilled and cubed
¾ cup (185ml) water

Combine the flour and salt in a large bowl. Use your fingertips to rub the butter into the flour until the mixture resembles fine breadcrumbs. Add the water to the flour mixture and use a knife in a cutting motion to mix until the mixture just comes together, slowly add extra water if the mixture is a little dry until you have a soft dough. Use your hands to bring the mixture together.

Turn the dough onto a lightly floured surface and knead gently for 1–2 minutes or until smooth. Shape the dough into a soft smooth ball and place into the camp oven. You can line the bottom of your camp oven with baking paper. Cook for approximately 30 minutes or until the damper is cooked through.

Bacon Bones
Soupy Stewy Thing

About 1kg bacon bones

1L chicken stock

500ml or so of ginger beer/ginger ale

500ml lite sour cream (optional)

3–4 potatoes, roughly chopped

1 small sweet potato, roughly chopped

3–4 celery stalks, chopped

2–3 capsicum cheeks, finely chopped

2 carrots, chopped

1 brown onion, chopped

2–3 field mushrooms, chopped

1 large red chilli, finely chopped

1 can creamed corned

1 can super sweet corn kernels

Handful or two of tube pasta

½ cup soup mix (peas, barley, lentils)

Splash of Bundy

Add whatever you like to taste: chilli, garlic, ginger, salt, pepper, black sauce, brown sugar, maple syrup to sweeten

It's just a matter of chucking it all in the camp oven and keeping an eye on it. You can pre-fry some of the mushrooms/onion/chilli if you like. You can also add or subtract anything you like. Taste as you go. Just remember you can always add more, you can't take it out. Serve with sourdough and butter or mashed potatoes.

Ham Bone Soup with Leek and Red Lentils

Oil

1 ham bone

2 leeks

2 potatoes, peeled and chopped

2 carrots, peeled and chopped

3 garlic cloves, crushed

1 cup red lentils (or split peas)

1L vegetable stock

Note: Add your own favourite vegetables, herbs and spices.

Heat the oil in the camp oven, add the bone, all the vegetables and garlic, frying off for a few minutes. Add the lentils and stock and cook until the meat falls off the bone.

CANOLA CROPS NEAR COWRA

Nature's colours can't be captured in their purity and glow,
It's a thought that tortures artists, as only artists know,
While the scene is rich and vivid in a rich and fertile mind
On the journey to the canvas something special's left behind
But I'll share with you an image that will never go away,
The canola crops near Cowra on a warm September day.

We headed out from Canberra for south-west New South Wales
With the old colt, Billy Rowlands, fertilising bushman's tales
And he's got a way of speaking the country folk know well,
'Colt, six weeks ago out here the place was dry as hell
'But then we got the rain like I thought we bloody would
'And colt, there's canola crops out here that are pretty bloody good.'

As I absorbed the Old Colt's character the miles quickly passed,
Laughter silenced silence and each yarn was his last,
The scent of spring was heavy on a fresh and gentle breeze
That gave away its presence as it danced its way through trees,
Then came forth the vision that took my breath away,
The canola crops near Cowra on a warm September day.

Like a dangerous hue of gold that alters minds and fathers dreams
It was oozing over fence lines, paddocks bursting at the seams,
A patchwork-quilted countryside hypnotising passers-by,
A sun-kissed magic melody composed by earth and sky,
And as I go through life I'll remember all the way
The canola crops near Cowra on a warm September day.

Murray Hartin

THE VEGIE PATCH, PIES AND PASTRY

Baked Cauliflower

1 cauliflower
1 tbsp butter
2 tbsp olive oil
½ tbsp salt
¼ tsp pepper
2 garlic cloves, crushed
2/3 tbsp Parmesan cheese
Fresh parsley, finely chopped

Wash the cauliflower and remove the leaves. In a small bowl whisk together the butter, oil, salt, pepper and crushed garlic. Place the cauliflower in a camp oven and completely coat it with the seasoning mix. Cover with foil and cook for 30 minutes then remove the foil and cook for a further 10–20 minutes. Sprinkle with Parmesan cheese and cook until melted then sprinkle with parsley and serve. You can also use broccoli if you like!

Vegie Stew with Cheddar Cheese Dumplings

2 tbsp olive oil

3 carrots, chopped

3 leeks, chopped

3 garlic cloves, minced

3 tbsp plain flour

1L vegetable stock

2 zucchinis, chopped

2 x 400g cans cannelloni beans

1 bay leaf

4 thyme and rosemary sprigs

200ml sour cream

1 tbsp whole grain mustard

200g baby spinach

Fresh parsley

Dumplings

50g butter

100g self-raising flour

100g grated mature cheese

Parsley

To make the dumplings, fold/rub the butter into the flour, add cheese and parsley and fold through. Form into balls a bit smaller than a tennis ball.

To make the stew, add olive oil to the camp oven then cook the carrots. When softened add the leeks and minced garlic. Add flour and slowly add vegetable stock, stirring so there are no lumps. Add the remaining ingredients and simmer on low heat. Add the dumplings and cook for 1 hour. Note: cooking time may vary depending on heat.

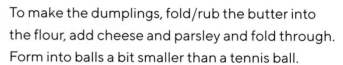

Guinness Pot Pie

2kg chuck steak, diced

1 tbsp oil

3 onions, sliced

4 garlic cloves, crushed

2/3 cup plain flour

400ml Guinness beer

2 cups beef stock

Ready rolled puff pastry

1 egg, beaten

Brown the steak in hot oil then remove from the oven and set aside. Cook the onions and garlic in the camp oven then sprinkle in the flour and cook for 1 minute. Return the meat to the oven and add Guinness and stock and simmer for a couple of hours until the sauce has thickened. Pop the puff pastry over the top and brush with the beaten egg mixture. Fit the camp oven lid and put coals on top and cook until golden, about 25 minutes. Just very tasty. We teamed the pie up with any vegies left in the fridge and a couple of potatoes, lots of garlic and a bit of cream.

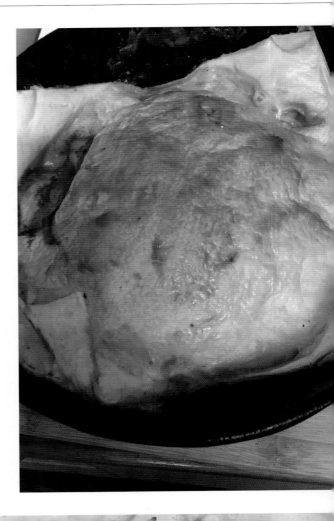

Savoury Beef Roll

500g beef mince
1½ cups breadcrumbs
1 onion, finely chopped
1½ cups grated carrot
1½ cups finely chopped green capsicum
1½ cups finely chopped celery
2 beef stock cubes
2 tbsp Worcestershire sauce
3 tbsp tomato paste
1/3 tsp lemon pepper
2 tbsp chopped parsley
3 sheets frozen puff pastry
Beaten egg for glazing

Quickly fry off the mince for 1–2 minutes in a hot pan then set aside to cool for 10 minutes. Combine the mince, breadcrumbs, vegies, beef stock cubes, Worcestershire sauce, tomato paste, pepper and parsley and mix well. Put the mixture into the middle of the pastry and fold over and join the edges. Brush the edges with water to make them stick. Brush over with egg white and cook until golden brown.

Chicken and Fennel Pie

750g chicken thigh fillets

1 tbsp oil

2 fennel bulbs, tops cut off and fennel heart sliced up

1 carrot, cut into small pieces

1 leek, cut into rounds

2 large mushrooms, cut into small pieces

2 celery stalks, cut into small pieces

3 garlic cloves, chopped

1 red chilli (seeds in), chopped

1 tsp fennel seeds

Splash of white wine

3 tbsp plain flour

¾ cup chicken stock

¾ cup cream

¾ cup milk

4 tarragon stems (leaves only, do not place the stalks into the mixture)

Chives

1 sheet puff pastry

1 egg

1 tbsp extra milk

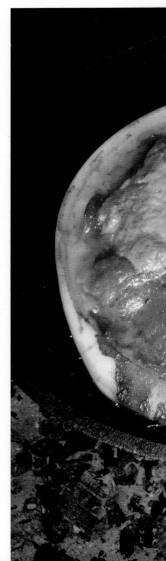

Cube the chicken fillets into about 2cm pieces and cook in oil until just cooked. Remove the chicken from the pan and place in a separate bowl.

Add (to the same pan) the fennel, carrot, leek, mushrooms, celery, garlic and chilli. Cook, stirring often, for about 10 minutes until the vegetables are almost cooked. Return the chicken to the pan and mix together.

Add the fennel seeds and white wine. Add the plain flour and stir to coat the chicken and vegetables, stir for about 1 minute to cook the flour.

Raise the heat to medium-high and add the chicken stock, cream, milk, tarragon and chives, allow to simmer gently, stirring often until the mixture thickens. Season with salt and pepper to taste.

Place the mixture in an oven proof dish.

In a small bowl mix the egg and extra milk with a fork. Brush the top edges of the oven proof dish with the egg mixture. Lay the pastry over the dish and gently press the overhanging edges of pastry so they stick to the sides of the dish. Lightly brush more of the egg mixture over the pastry and sprinkle with salt. Cut 4 small slits in the pastry.

Cook in the camp oven low and slow for about 30–40 minutes or until the puff pastry is a deep golden brown and puffed.

Puffy Dogs For The Kids

A great cook the kids can take part in.

Packet of 10 frankfurts
1 packet of puff pastry
1 packet of grated cheese
1 onion, diced
Tomato sauce
Milk

Quarter 3 sheets of puff pastry with a knife. Place a frankfurt on a quarter sheet of pastry and wrap with cheese and onion then close
off both ends. Brush with milk and place on a trivet lined with baking paper in a camp oven over medium heat, cook while continuously turning for about 20 minutes until golden brown. A trivet and low heat is required or the pastry will quickly burn. Serve on a platter with tomato sauce.

Pork, Fennel and Apple Sausage Rolls

1 large fennel bulb

2 large carrots, peeled

2 green apples

Olive oil spray

500g lean pork mince

¾ cup fresh wholegrain breadcrumbs

2 eggs

1 tbsp Dijon mustard

2 sheets frozen puff pastry, thawed

1 tsp fennel seeds, crushed

1 cup continental parsley, leaves picked

2 tsp olive oil

Preheat the camp oven. Place a trivet lined with baking paper in the bottom of it.

Trim and reserve the fennel fronds. Halve the bulb and grate one half, reserving the other half. Finely grate half a carrot and 1 apple.

Heat a large non-stick pan over medium-high heat. Spray with oil, add grated vegetables and apple and cook for 8 minutes or until the liquid has evaporated. Transfer to a large bowl and cool.

Add the mince, breadcrumbs, 1 egg and mustard to the vegetable mixture. Season and mix together well.

Cut the pastry sheets in half. Shape ¼ of the mince mixture into a log the same length as the pastry. Place onto the pastry and roll over to enclose the filling. Repeat with the remaining mixture. Cut each roll into 4 pieces.

Transfer the sausage rolls to the trivet. Beat the remaining egg in a small bowl. Brush the rolls with the egg and sprinkle with fennel seeds. Bake on low heat for up to 40 minutes or until puffed and golden. Serve sausage rolls with anything you want.

Filo pastry

3 cups (450g) plain flour, plus extra for dusting
1/3 cup olive oil, plus extra for drizzling
1 tsp salt
½ tsp white sugar
1 cup water

Filling

1 bunch
of spinach
2 tbsp salt
250g feta
100g ricotta
2 eggs
2 tsp dill leaves, chopped
1 tbsp mint leaves, chopped
Pinch of white pepper
Note: you can add spicy sausage to heat the filling up.

To make the filo, place the flour in a large bowl. Add the olive oil and using your hands, rub through the flour until completely combined. Add the salt, sugar and water, stir to form a loose dough. Add more water if necessary. Turn the dough out on a floured surface and knead for 10 minutes or until soft and elastic. Return to the bowl then cover and rest for 10 minutes. Note: or use pre-made filo pastry, six layers for each roll.

To make the filling, steam the spinach then squeeze the excess water from it. Place the spinach in a bowl with the feta, ricotta, eggs, herbs and pepper. Stir to combine and set aside.

Divide the dough into three even pieces. Place one piece of dough on a floured surface. Using a rolling pin, roll out the dough to form a circle. Continue rolling, lightly dusting with flour between each roll, until 2mm thick (roughly 50cm diameter). Drizzle a little oil over the filo and place one-third of the spinach mixture at one end, leaving a 3cm border. Gently roll up the filo to enclose the filling, ensuring it is shaped like a coil. Place in a greased and foil-lined camp oven.

Repeat the process with the remaining dough and filling, placing the coils in separate pans. Generously brush oil over the coils and bake for 45 minutes or until golden.

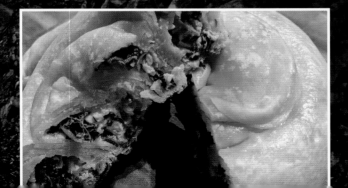

Homemade Sausage rolls

3 x sausage mince rolls from Woollies (ya know like the Devon rolls but sausage mince)

1 x 6 pack puff pastry sheets

1 tbsp mixed herbs

1 tbsp oregano

1 tbsp garlic granules

1 tbsp thyme leaves

½ tbsp chilli flakes

Eggs

Milk

10–13g fennel seeds

Grated cheese

Sesame seeds

Generally just what you have in the cupboard but the secret ingredient you MUST include is fennel seeds. Don't be scared to use at least half a 26g jar of these sausage-flavouring beauties plus grated cheese.

Lay the frozen sheets of pastry out on the bench to defrost. In a big bowl mix the rest of the ingredients together. Do not forget those fennel seeds.

Divide the mixture into even portions for as many pastry sheets you have and roll each portion into a log. Pop each log on one edge of the pastry sheets and roll those tasty morsels into a sausage roll.

Cut into 3–4 each and place into the camp oven on a baking paper lined trivet, keeping a bit of space between each.

Grab some eggs and milk to knock up an egg wash and either brush it on top or if you are lazy just pour it over. Sprinkle some sesame seeds over and place on the coals and cover with coals. You are looking for a fairly hot temperature to roast.

Keep an eye on it and in about 45 minutes and they should be ready to smash. Enjoy!

Mathew Donaldson, 15, is the Great Coronavirus Camp Oven Cook Off group's youngest and most consistent enthusiast. While he struggles a tad with high-resolution pictures of all his creations, he burns the coals every weekend and has come up with some great plates of food. He hadn't used a camp oven before the Facebook page was created but is now 'hooked on that feeling'. The Mackay (Queensland) larrikin lives to fish for Barra and barrack for his beloved Newcastle Knights in the NRL. Camp oven cooking is now No.3 on his weekly 'to do' list and here is his unique take on how to go about camp oven cooking through the eyes of a 15-year-old. 'The Little Champ' writes his own self-crafted recipes. Gold.

Hornsby Fire Brigade 50
Join in Camp Oven Cook Off

A couple of weeks into the Great Coronavirus Cook Off, Hornsby 50 Fire Station crew members had some down-time while on duty on the outskirts of Sydney.

After watching the Facebook page grow, Jiya Reardon decided he would cook lunch for the troops in the camp oven at the station and it ended up as a combined effort using butane burners. Halfway through the cook the alarms went off and Station 50 was called to a job.

'I just turned off the burners thinking that it may be the end of a great idea and off we went sirens blazing,' said Jiya. 'It was only a false alarm, so we returned to base, turned on the gas and the feed was sensational.

'It was a first-time experience for many of the crew and many have since purchased camp ovens and are cooking full steam ahead and loving it.'

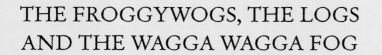

THE FROGGYWOGS, THE LOGS
AND THE WAGGA WAGGA FOG

One day in Wagga Wagga the Froggywogs got bogged
In their red rust-bucket truck that was loaded up with logs,
They were flying through the fog when they swerved to miss a dog
And now the Froggywogs were bogged in the Wagga Wagga fog.

The logs bogged in the fog were for the Buzztown Bees
They'd rung the Froggywogs and said *'We'd like some logs now, please,'*
'Our firewood's run out and it's minus 3 degrees!'
Unless the Frogs un-bogged the logs the Buzztown Bees would freeze!

Things were looking hopeless but the Froggywogs struck luck,
Fearless Freddie Flying Fox and Dangerous Dudley Duck
Were heading to Temora in the Shire Fire-truck
And somehow through the fog they could see the Frogs were stuck.

'We'll get you out,' yelled Fred, he had a lot of brains,
'All you have to do is hook up to this chain'.
They quickly pulled them out just as it began to rain
And pretty soon the Froggywogs were on the road again.

The Buzztown Bees, they didn't freeze, they finally got their logs
Thanks to Fearless Fred and Dudley and of course the Froggywogs.
Who still laugh about the time when they swerved to miss a dog
And bogged a load of logs in the Wagga Wagga fog.

Murray Hartin

SWEET
TREATS

Ma Ma's Caramel Apple Pie

Caramel

1 cup brown sugar

1 tbsp butter

1 cup milk

1 tbsp plain flour

2 egg yolks

1 tsp vanilla

Sweet butter crust

1¼ cup plain flour

1 tbsp sugar

½ cup unsalted butter,
cold and cubed

4 tbsp ice cold water

Apples, peeled and sliced

Milk

Sugar

For the caramel, boil all ingredients together over medium heat, stirring constantly. When the mixture is smooth, cool in the fridge.

For the sweet butter crust, in an electric mixer fitted with the paddle attachment, mix together the flour, sugar and butter until small pieces form. Add water slowly and mix until incorporated.

Wrap the dough in cling wrap and place in the fridge until ready to use.

After rolling out the dough, pour the cooled caramel in the centre and place finely sliced apples on top. Turn the edges of the pastry in to form a pie. Brush with milk and sprinkle with raw sugar.

Place on a trivet in a camp oven and bake over coals with some also placed on top.

Keep a close eye on it as it can burn very quickly. Bake for 15 minutes to start with and then check every couple of minutes after that until cooked. Serve with cream or ice cream. Note: If you don't want to use fresh apples you can use tinned!

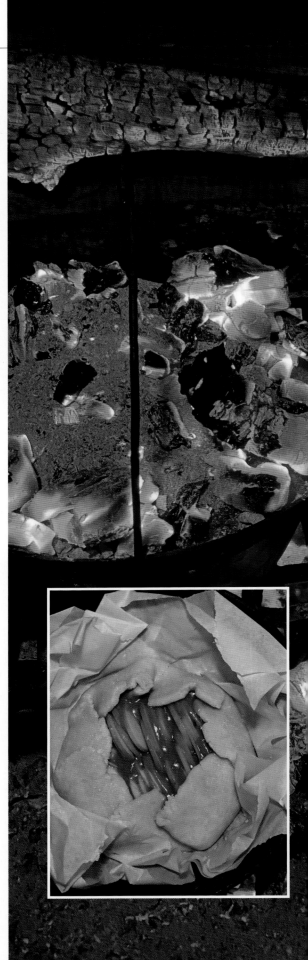

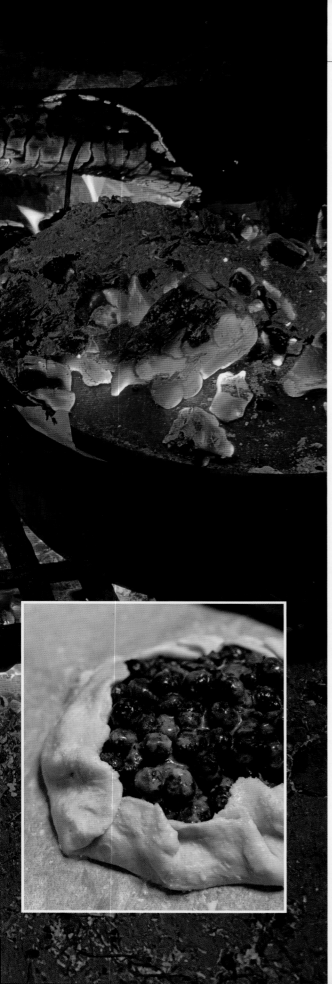

Blueberry and Lavender Pie

Sweet butter crust

1¼ cup plain flour

1 tbsp sugar

½ cup unsalted butter, cold and cubed

4 tbsp ice-cold water

Blueberry filling

½ cup sugar

3 tbsp cornflour

½ tsp dried lavender

4 cups fresh blueberries

2 tbsp unsalted butter, melted

In an electric mixer fitted with the paddle attachment, mix together the flour, sugar and butter until small pieces form. Add the water in slowly and mix until incorporated. Wrap the dough in cling wrap and place in the fridge until ready to use.

Whisk together the sugar, cornflour and dried lavender in a large stainless steel bowl. Add the blueberries and butter. Crush a few berries with the back of a spatula and mix until the flour and berries are coated. Let sit for 15 minutes, stirring occasionally.

Remove the dough from the fridge, place on baking paper and roll out into a circle. Place the berries in a pile in the centre of the dough, fold the edges around to make the pie, brush with milk and sprinkle with raw sugar.

Place on a trivet lined with baking paper in a camp oven and bake over coals with some on top also. Keep a close eye on it as it can burn very quickly. Bake for 15 minutes to start with and then check every couple of minutes after that until cooked.

Serve with cream or ice cream. Enjoy!

Super Scones (Savoury and Plain)

Fill the camp oven half plain and the other half savoury to keep everyone happy.

Plain

3 cups flour
Pinch of salt
1 cup cream
1 cup lemonade*
Jam and cream to serve

Savoury

1 cup chopped bacon
1 tsp mixed herbs
1 cup of mixed cheeses (e.g. Parmesan and cheddar)
Butter to serve

Note: Lemon, lime and bitters is a good alternative to lemonade. Add chopped onion, garlic or any spicy flavours for the savoury scones.

Mix the flour and salt in a bowl. Make a well in the centre and pour in the cream and fizzy drink. Bring together to form a soft dough, gently knead and divide the mixture in half. Put the plain dough into one side of the camp oven with a little foil to separate. Work through the savoury ingredients into the remaining dough and place on the other side of the oven. Cut the scones into preferred sizes and brush with oil or milk before cooking. Cook on a layer of foil until the scones starts to turn golden brown.

Strawberry and Almond Frangipani Braid

¾ cup almond meal
45g cold butter or coconut oil
3 tbsp raw sugar or Demerara Sugar, plus extra for sprinkling
1 tsp vanilla
1 egg
1 sheet pastry
200g strawberries, diced

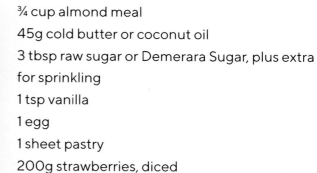

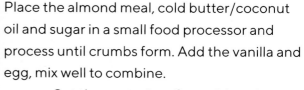

Place the almond meal, cold butter/coconut oil and sugar in a small food processor and process until crumbs form. Add the vanilla and egg, mix well to combine.

Cut the pastry into 2cm wide strips down both sides of the sheet. Spread the mixture down the middle of the pastry then top with diced strawberries. Working from top to bottom, lift the pastry so it overlaps each other. Brush with egg so it browns. Once done sprinkle with extra sugar.

Put it into your camp oven on a trivet lined with baking paper. Put some coals on the bottom but not too many because you don't want to burn the bottom of your pastry, just enough to brown it. Place more on the lid to get it cooking on top and to get it nice and brown. Serve with ice cream or cream.

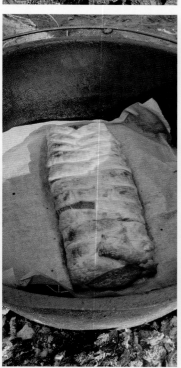

Apple Cinnamon Scrumptious Custard Scrolls

Dough

2 cups self-raising flour

2 tbsp butter

½ cup milk

Cinnamon spread

½ cup butter

½ cup brown sugar

1 tsp cinnamon

1 cup cooked apple

Custard

1 cup milk

2 eggs

2 tbsp sugar

½ tsp vanilla essence

Sift the flour into a bowl, cut the butter into cubes and rub into the flour. Slowly add the milk and mix to form a soft dough. Press out to 1cm thickness.

For the spread, mix the butter, brown sugar and cinnamon together. Spread over the dough then add the apple on top. Roll up and cut into 2cm pieces.

Grease a bundt tin and place the rounds in it.

Prepare the custard by mixing milk, sugar, vanilla and eggs together. Pour over the scrolls.

Place a trivet in the bottom of a camp oven and put the cake tin in. Fill the camp over with water halfway up and put the lid on. Cook for 40 minutes in the fire with coals on top.

Waffle Cone Desserts

Many great evenings were had by our campfire. Thank you so much for keeping us going through this crazy time. This group has really helped bring back the value of family time and the joys of cooking in our own backyards!

Waffles cones
Mini marshmallows
Fresh or frozen berries
Chocolate chips
Banana (although we forgot to add this in ours)

Fill the cones with all the ingredients, layered in any order (kids loved this!). Cover in foil and place on a campfire hotplate for up to 5 minutes (we turned them after 3 minutes). Check the cones to see if the marshmallows and chocolate have melted. Enjoy!

Apple Pies

These mini apple pies are super easy to make. Simply use one apple per person you're cooking for.

Granny Smith apples
Sugar
1 sheet of puff pastry (plus more if needed)
Hershey's Caramel Sauce
Chocolate of choice

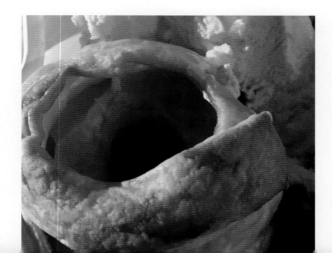

Peel the apples and core out the centre using a melon baller, but don't go all the way through. Leave about 1cm in the bottom of each apple. Roll the apple in sugar.

Cut the sheet of puff pastry into 2.5cm strips. Start at the bottom and wrap around the apple, joining the pieces as you go.

Place a piece of chocolate inside each apple and fill with caramel sauce.

Place the apples in the camp oven. Place the oven on coals and put a good shovel full of coals on the lid of the closed oven. Check after 20 minutes then continue cooking and check again after an additional 10 minutes. Ours took 30 minutes to cook. Enjoy!

Baklava

500g walnuts, crumbled
(or use pistachios and walnuts)
2 tsp cinnamon
1 packet of filo pastry
385g unsalted butter, melted

Syrup
¾ cup sugar
2 tbsp lemon juice
1 cup honey
1 cup water

Mix the nuts and cinnamon. Working with one filo sheet at a time, add to the camp oven and paint with the butter, repeat for 5 sheets then spread ¾ cup of the nut mixture over. Add another 5 sheets of pastry painted with butter then spread ¾ cup of the nut mixture, repeat 3 times in all. Finish with 10 layers of pastry each painted with butter. Bake for 45–60 minutes over a low heat camp oven. Keep an eye on it.

For the syrup, stir together the sugar, lemon juice, honey and water. Heat until all dissolved and let cool. Pour over the Baklava and let set for 6 hours or overnight. Enjoy.

Stuffed Bananas in Foil

Go bananas over this dessert! It's super easy for young and old to make. There are two types of fillings below but get as creative as you like.

Bananas
Old Gold Caramel chocolate
Marshmallows
Desiccated coconut
Frozen mixed berries (thawed)
Custard or ice cream to serve

Slice the banana (skin on) on the inside curve with a knife, careful not to cut through the bottom of the peel. You can then fill with toppings of your choice. For one we did Old Gold caramel chocolate (3 squares per banana) with mixed berries and sprinkled with coconut, and another with the caramel chocolate, marshmallows and coconut. Just wrap in foil and put in the camp oven on medium coals for around 20–30 minutes. When ready, open the bananas and serve with some vanilla custard on top.

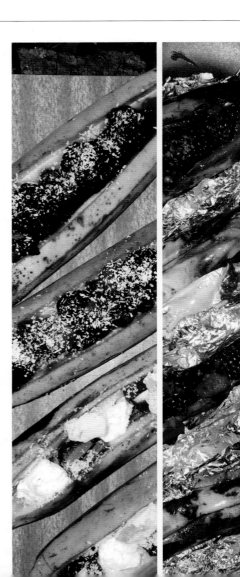